CONTENTS

Introduction; conventions   v

Scientific names   1

Those scientific names from the addenda and
corrigenda which are not in the main body of
the index   37

English names   38

List of abbreviations of authors' names   52

Addenda and corrigenda   56

A Recorder's Log Book or Label List of

BRITISH BUTTERFLIES AND MOTHS

J. D. Bradley and D. S. Fletcher

INDEX

Compiled by D. H. Hall-Smith

together with
ADDENDA AND CORRIGENDA
Compiled by J. D. Bradley and D. S. Fletcher

LEICESTERSHIRE MUSEUMS SERVICE
1983

Leicestershire Museums Publication No. 41
ISBN 0 85022 120 X
Printed by Reprographics Section, Leicestershire County Council

INTRODUCTION

When using *A Recorder's Log Book or Label List* I found that a considerable amount of time was spent finding species to which I wanted to refer and I therefore, with the agreement of Dr. Bradley and Mr. Fletcher, decided to compile an index. They have also provided addenda and corrigenda so as to bring the *Log Book* up to date.

I have also had enquiries from amateur lepidopterists regarding the abbreviations of authors' names and have included an indexed list of them.

Please inform me of any corrections.

D.H. Hall-Smith
Leicestershire Museums Service, 96 New Walk, Leicester LE1 6TD

CONVENTIONS

Typography

The following type faces have been used:

> FAMILY
> SUBFAMILY
> Genus
> species
> English Names
> *All synonyms in italics*

Homonyms

With scientific names the specific name is followed by the generic name except that when they are in the same genus the author's name is appended.

With English homonymous names the scientific names are appended.

SCIENTIFIC NAMES

A

abbreviana   1150
abbreviata   1852
abdominalis   406
abietana   1059
abietaria   1815
abietella   1454
Abraxas   1884
Abrostola   2449
abruptaria   1936
abscisana   1108
absinthiata   1830
absinthii   2211

acanthadactyla   1497
Acanthophila   851
Acanthopsyche   191
Acasis   1883
accentifera   2431
Acentria   1331
acerbella   997
aceriana   1167
aceris, Acronicta   2279
aceris, Stigmella   102
acetosae   118
acetosellae   2141
achatana   1115
Acherontia   1973
ACHIEARINAE   1661
Achlya   1659
Achroia   1426
Acigona   1291
Acleris   1038
Acontia   2415
Acompsia   855
Acosmetia   2393
Acrobasis   1435
Acrocercops   311
Acrolita   1160
Acrolepia   476
ACROLEPIINAE   471
Acrolepiopsis   473
Acronicta   2278
ACRONICTINAE   2277
acroxantha   656
acteon   1528
Actinotia   2097
acuminatana   1279
acuminatella   822
acuta   2429

Adaina   1517
Adela   149

ADELINAE   144
adippe   1606
adjunctella   586
Adoxophyes   999
Adscita   163
adscitella   622
adspersella   567
adusta   2250
adustata   1888
advenaria   1901
advenella   1439

aegeria   1614
aegrotalis   1407
aemula   2486
aemulana   1194
aenaena   952
aeneella   100
aeneofasciella   55
aequidentellus   484
aeratana   1287
aeretella   486
aeriferanus   987
aerugula   2079
aescularia   1663
aestivaria   1669
aestivella   725
Aethalura   1951
Aethes   939
aethiops, Erebia   1618
aethiops, Xenolechia   763

affinitana   932
affinitatum   1802
affinis, Bryotropha   779
affinis, Cosmia   2316

Agapeta   937
agathina   2135
AGDISTINAE   1487
Agdistis   1487
agestis   1572
Aglais   1593
aglaja   1607
Aglossa   1420
agnotana   1226
Agonopterix   688
agrimoniae   26
Agriopis   1932
Agriphila   1303
Agrius   1971
Agrochola   2262
Agrotera   1410
Agrotis   2084

ahenella, Coleophora 514
ahenella, Hypochalcia 1457

Alabonia 652
ulacella 851
albedinella 271
albersana 1217
albiceps 756
albicilla 1446
albicillata 1748
albicolon 2152
albicomella 204
albicosta 544
albidella, Biselachista 630
albidella, Coleophora 532
albifasciella 37
albifrontella 601
albimaculata 2172
albipaepella 848
albipuncta 2194
albipunctata 1677
albipunctella, Depressaria 680
albipunctella, Nemapogon 217
albistria 422
albovenosa 2290
albuginana 1229
albula 2076
albulata, Asthena 1875
albulata, Perizoma 1807
alburnella 771
alceae 1533
alchemillata 1803
alchimiella 286
alchymista 2464
alciphron 1565
Alcis 1941
alcyonipennella 517
Aleimma 1032
Aleucis 1959
alexis 1579
algae, Archanara 2374
algae, Cryphia 2292
algira 2460
alismana 930
Alispa 1465
allisella 687
Allophyes 2245
alnetella 115
alni 2281
alniaria 1913
alnifoliae 498
alnifoliella, auct. 344
alnifoliella, Hb. 345
alpella 458
alpicola, Parornix 306
alpicola, Xestia 2125

alpinalis 1394
alpinana 1274
alpinella, Elachista 599
alpinella, Platytes 1325
alpium 2277
alsinella 827
alsines 2381
Alsophila 1663
alstroemeriana 695
alternana 935
alternaria 1890
alternata 1738
alternella 1025
alticolella 584
Alucita 1288
ALUCITIDAE 1288

ambigua 2384
ambigualis 1334
ambiguella 955
Amblyptilia 1497
amethystina 2310
Amphipoea 2357
Amphipyra 2297
AMPHIPYRINAE 2296
Amphisbatis 659
amplana 1262

Anacampsis 852
anachoreta 2018
Anania 1381
Anaplectoides 2138
Anarsia 856
Anarta 2142
anatipennella 533
anceps, Apamea 2333
anceps, Peridea 2005
ancilla 2071
Ancylis 1115
Ancylolomia 1327
Ancylosis 1467
anderidae 347
Anerastia 1432
angelicella, Agonopterix 713
angelicella, Parornix 303
Angerona 1924
angulifasciella 28
angulipennis 1352
angustalis 1414
angustana 954
angustea 1342
angustella 1465
angusticolella 127
angusticostella 213
angustiorana 1010

angustipennis 206
anisalis 1397
annulata 1676
annulatella auct. 565
annulatella Nyl. 572
annulatella, Rhigognostis 467
anomala 2394
anomalella 92
Anomis 2471
Anthocharis 1553
Anthophila 385
anthracinalis 197
anthraciniformis 378
anthyllidella 843
Antichloris 2073
Anticlea 1746
Anticollix 1863
Antigastra 1400
antiopa 1596
antiqua 2026
Antispila 158
antistacta 279
Antitype 2254

Apamea 2321
Apatura 1585
Apeira 1910
Aphantopus 1629
Aphelia 988
Aphomia 1428
aphrodite 1604
apicella 1129
apicipunctella 602
apiformis 370
Aplasta 1664
Aplocera 1867
Aplota 653
Apocheima 1925
Apoda 173
Apodia 730
apollo 1536
Apomyelois 1486
Aporia 1548
Aporophyla 2230
Apotomis 1089
applana 688
aprica 2416
aprilina 2247
Aproarema 843

aquata 1783

Arashnia 1599
arbutella 1071

arcella, Argyresthia 414
arcella, Nemapogon 220
arceuthina 405
Archarana 2370
ARCHIEARINAE 1661
Archiearis 1661
Archinemapogon 222
Archips 976
Arctia 2057
ARCTIIDAE 2035
Arctornis 2032
arctostaphyli 508
arcuatella, Ectoedemia 30
arcuella 1080
ardeaepennella 535
arenaria 1946
arenella 687
Arenipses 1431
Arenostola 2377
areola 2243
arethusa 1624
Arethusana 1624
argentana 1028
argentea 2212
argentella, Elachista 610
argentella, Psamathrocrita 750a
argentimaculella 203
argentipedella 34
argentula 563
argiades 1570
argiolus 1580
Argolamprotes 734
argus 1571
Argynnis 1603
argyrana 1228
argyrella 1448
Argyresthia 401
ARGYRESTHIINAE 401
argyropeza 23
Argyrotaenia 974
Aricia 1574
aridella 1324
arion 1581
aristella 655
Aristotelia 751
armigera 2400
armoricanus 1535
Aroga 796
artaxerxes 1573
artemisiae 2213
artemisicolella 577
artemisiella, Bucculatrix 269
artemisiella, Coleophora 576
artemisiella, Scrobipalpa 820
aruncella 4
arundinata 1333
arundinetella 744

asella 174
ashworthii 2129
asperella 454
aspersana 1043
aspidiscana 1190
Aspilapteryx 294
Aspitates 1967
Assara 1461
assectella 473
assimilata 1832
assimilella, Agonopterix 702
assimilella, Stigmella 74
asteris, Coleophora 562
asteris, Cucullia 2217
Asthena 1875
astrantiae 712

atalanta 1590
Ateliotum 208
Atemelia 448
Atethmia 2269
athalia 1613
Athetis 2392
Atolmis 2039
atomaria 1952
atra, Acanthopsyche 191
atra, Blastodacna 906
atrata 1870
atrella 731
atricapitana 966
atricapitella 83
atricollis 29
atricomella 597
atrifrontella 41
atripicella 818
atriplicis, Coleophora 573
atriplicis, Trachea 2304
atropos 1973
atropunctana 1085

aucupariae 103
Augasma 486
augur 2114
augustella 638
aurago 2272
aurana 1272
aurantiana 1233
aurantiaria 1933
aurata 1361
aureatella 3
aurella 50
auricoma 2287
aurinia 1610
auritella, Opostega 120
auritella, Stigmella 69

aurofasciana 1069
auroguttella 297
auromarginella 54
aurulentella 408
ausonia 1554
australis, Aporophyla 2230
australis, Colias 1544
Autographa 2441
autumnaria 1911
autumnata 1797
Auximobasis 876

avellana 173
avellanella 666
aversata 1713

Axylia 2098

azaleella 285

B

Bacotia 183
Bactra 1110
badiana 1126
badiata 1746
badiella 674
badiipennella 497
baja 2130
bajularia 1667
baliodactylus 1512
balteolella 399
Bankesia 182
bankesiella 1456
bankiana 2413
basaltinella 777
basiguttella 89
basistrigalis 1334a
Batia 640
batis 1652
Batrachedra 878
BATRACHEDRINAE 878

beatricella 951
bedellella 616
Bedellia 264
BEDELLIINAE 264
bella 2055
bellargus 1576
Bembecia 382
bembeciformis 371

Bena 2421
benanderi 565
bennetii 1488
berbera 2298
berberata 1785
bergamanniana 1035
betulae, Heliozela 157
betulae, Metriostola 1450
betulae, Parornix 301
betulae, Thecla 1556
betulana 978
betularia 1931
betulella 474
betuletana 1093
betulicola, Caloptilia 283
betulicola, Stigmella 110
betulina 188
betulinella 223

biangulata 1793
biatomella 595
bicolorata 2164
bicoloria 2012
bicostella 654
bicruris 2173
bicuspis 1996
bidentata 1920
bifasciana, Olethreutes 1079
bifasciana, Spatalistis 1034
bifasciata 1804
bifida 1998
bifractella 730
bigella 1472
bilinealis 1353
bilineata 1742
biloba 2445
bilunana 1133
bimaculata, Autographa 2446
bimaculata, Lomographa 1957
bimaculosa 2244
binaevella 1483
binaria 1646
binderella 512
biplaga 2419
bipunctaria 1731
bipunctella 720
bipunctidactyla 1508
bipunctosa 699
biren 2162
biriviata 1721
Biselachista 624
biselata 1702
Bisigna 639
bisontella 252
bisselliella 236
Biston 1930

bistorata 1947
bistriatella 1486
bistriga 1433
bistrigella 128
bisulcella 623
Bithrys 2180

bjerkandrella 386

blabcardella 326
blanda 2382
blandella, Brachmia 866
blandella, Caryocolum 832
blandiata 1806
blandulella 835
Blastesthia 1208
BLASTOBASIDAE 873
Blastobasis 873
Blastodacna 905
BLASTODACNINAE 902
blattariella 854
blenna 2161
Blepharita 2249
blomeri 1872

Boarmia 1943
boeticus 1567
Bohemannia 19
boisduvaliella 1453
Boloria 1600
bombycina 2148
boreella 783
borelii 2365
Borkhausenia 644
borreonella 205
boscana 1050
boteli 196
botrana 1107
bowesi 1521

Brachionycha 2227
Brachmia 866
Brachylomia 2225
bractea 2444
bractella 651
bradfordi 33
branderiana 1088
brassicae, Mamestra 2154
brassicae, Pieris 1549
brevilinea 2351
briseis 1623
britanniodactyla 1494
brizella 753

brockeella 410
brongniardella 313
brumata 1799
brunnea 2122
brunnearia 1938
brunneata 1896
brunneella 675
brunnichana 1155
brunnichella 592
Bryotropha 777

BUCCULATRIGINAE 265
Bucculatrix 265
bucephala 1994
Buckleria 1493
buettneri 2376
buoliana 1210
Bupalus 1954

C

Cabera 1955
caca 2074
Cacoecimorpha 985
caecana 1240
caecimaculana 1188
Caenurgina 2458
caerulocephala 2020
caesia 2174
caesiata 1744
caesiella 437
caespititiella 587
cagnagella 427
caja 2057
Calamia 2366
Calamotropha 1292
c-album 1598
caledoniana 1040
calidella 1478
caliginosa 2393
Callimorpha 2068
Callistege 2462
Callisto 310
Callophrys 1555
Callopistria 2308
calodactyla 1500
Calophasia 2223
Caloptilia 280
calthella 5
Calybites 295
cambrica 1873
camilla 1584
Campaea 1961
campoliliana 1197

Camptogramma 1742
cana 1201
canella 1464
Canephora 193
caniola 2045
capitella 133
Capperia 1494
caprana 1154
caprealis 1420
capreana 1094
capreella 268
capreolella 715
caprimulgella 226
captiuncula 2344
capucina 2008
Caradrina 2387
carbonaria 1895
Carcacharodus 1533
Carcina 658
cardamines 1553
carduella 708
cardui 1591
carlinella 1485
carmelita 2010
carphodactyla 1519
carpinata 1881
carpinella 76
Carsia 1866
Carterocephalus 1525
Caryocolum 826
casta 186
castanea 2132
castaneae 160
castrensis 1635
Cataclysta 1354
catalaunalis 1400
Cataplectica 479
Catarhoe 1735
Catephia 2464
catharticella 98
Catocala 2451
CATOCALINAE 2451
Catoptria 1310
cauchiata 1829
cautella 1476
cavella 338

Cedestis 442
Celaena 2367
Celastrina 1580
celerio 1993
Celestica 206
Celphya 1063
cembrella 1332
CEMIOSTOMINAE 254
centaureata 1825

centifoliella 93
centrago 2269
centrostrigalis 1406
cephalonica 1427
Cephimallota 213
Cephitinea 214
Cepphis 1901
Ceramica 2163
Cerapteryx 2176
cerasana 970
cerasicolella 330
cerasivorella 495
Cerastis 2139
Ceratophaga 249
ceratoniae 1460
cerealella 749
Cerura 1995
cerusella 609
cerussella 1326
cervinalis 1788
cespitalis 1365
cespitana 1067
cespitis 2177

chaerophyllella 483
chalcites 2428
chalcogrammella 528
Chambersia 638
chamomillae 2214
Charadra 2426
Charanyca 2380
Cheimophila 665
chenopodiata 1732
Chesias 1864
chi 2254
Chilo 1290
Chilodes 2391
CHIMABACHINAE 663
Chionodes 790
chloerata 1859
CHLEOPHORINAE 2418
Chlorissa 1670
Chlorochlamys 1671
Chloroclysta 1760
Chloroclystis 1858
chloroleucaria 1671
chlorosata 1902
choragella 196
CHOREUTIDAE 385
Choreutis 387
Choristoneura 982
christyi 1796
chrysidiformis 384
chrysitis 2434
chrysocomae 1521
Chrysocrambus 1319

Chrysodeixis 2428
Chrysoesthia 746
chrysolepidella 7
chryson 2435
chrysonuchella 1321
CHRYSOPELEIINAE 908
chrysoprasaria 1673
chrysorrhoea 2029
Chrysoteuchia 1293

cicadella 919
cicatricella 1291
cidarella 272
Cidaria 1765
cilialis 1387
ciliella 689
Cilix 1651
cinctana 1005
cinctaria 1939
cinctella 849
cinerea 2084
cinerella 855
cinereopunctella 625
cinerosella 1469
cingillella 618
cingulata, Argrius 1971
cingulata, Pyrausta 1367
ciniflonella 686
cinnamomeana 971
cinxia 1612
circellaris 2262
circumflexa 1448
cirrigerella 1459
citrago 2271
citrana 1204
citrala 1762
citrinalis 657

clathrata 1894
clavaria 1745
Clavigesta 1206
clavipalpis 2389
clavis 2088
clementella 220
cleopatra 1547
Cleora 1939
Cleorodes 1945
Clepsis 991
clerkella 263
clintoni 817
cloacella 216
clorana 2418
Clostera 2017
clypeiferella 589

Clytie   2457

Cnaemidophorus   1496
Cnephasia   1016
cnicana   945
cnicella   690
cnicicolana   1185
c-nigrum   2126

COCHYLIDAE   921
Cochylidia   956
Cochylis   962
Coenobia   2379
Coenocalpe   1780
Coenonympha   1627
coenosa   2024
Coenotephria   1753
cognata   1770
cognatana   1265
Coleophora   489
COLEOPHORIDAE   486
COLIADINAE   1542
Colias   1542
Collicularia   1220
collitella   612
Colobochyla   2472
Colobura   1588
Colocasia   2425
colongella   214
Colostygia   1774
Colotois   1923
columbariella   239
comariana   1037
combinella   436
comes   2109
Comibaena   1667
comitata   1749
comma, Hesperia   1529
comma, Mythimna   2205
commoides   2207
Commophila   952
communana   1018
comparella   365
complana   2047
compositella   1241
compta   2170
comptana   1116
compunctella   439
concinnata   1763
conducta   2390
confusa, Hadena   2171
confusa, Macdunnoughia   2436
confusalis   2078
confusella   117
congelatella   1026

congressariella   839
conicolana   1269
coniferana   1268
conigera   2192
Conistra   2258
conjugella   418
consimilana   994
consociella   1437
consonaria   1949
consortana   1280
consortella   632
conspersana   1019
conspersella   739
conspicillaris   2181
conspicuella   539
conspurcatella   182
contaminella   1323
conterminana   1192
conterminella   710
contigua   2156
contiguaria   1710
continuella   64
conturbatella   885
convolvuli   1972
conwagana   1011
conyzae   521
coracina   1965
coracipenella   494
Corcyra   1427
cordigera   2143
coridon   1575
cornella   414
corollana   1270
coronata   1378
corticella   223
corylana   969
corylata   1773
coryli, Colocasia   2425
coryli, Phyllonorycter   342
corylifoliella   332
Coscinia   2053
Cosmia   2316
Cosmiotes   631
cosmophorana   1267
COSMOPTERIGINAE   894
Cosmopterix   894
Cosmorhoe   1752
COSSIDAE   160
COSSINAE   162
cossus   162
Costaconvexa   1741
costaestrigalis   2484
costalis   1413
costella   819
costipunctana   1187
costosa   706

8

craccae
CRAMBINAE 1289
Crambus 1294
Craniophora 2291
crassa 2094
crassalis 2476
crassiorella 187
crassiuscula 2458
crataegana 979
crataegella, Eudonia 1338
crataegella, Scythropia 450
crataegella, Stigmella 108
crataegi, Aporia 1548
crataegi, Bucculatrix 275
crataegi, Trichiura 1632
craterella 1320
cremiaria 1953
crenana 1149
crenata, Apamea 2326
crenata, Gluphisia 2016
crepuscularia 1948
crepusculella 121
cribraria 2053
cribrella 1458
cribrumalis 2493
crinanensis 2359
crini 2180
cristana 1054
cristatella 265
Crocallis 1921
crocicapitella 230
croceago 2257
crocealis 1385
croceus 1545
Crocidosema 1157
croesella 151
Croesia 1035
Crombrugghia 1491
cruciana 1147
cruda 2182
Cryphia 2292
cryptella 48
Cryptoblabes 1433
Cryptophlebia 1215

Ctenoplusia 2430
CTENUCHIDAE 2070

cuculata 1736
cuculipennella 280
cucullatella 2077
Cucullia 2211
CUCULLIINAE 2211
cucullina 2009
culiciformis 381

culmella, Agriphila 1304
culmella, Chrysoteuchia 1293
cultraria 1647
cuneatella 804
Cupido 1569
cuprella 149
cupriacella 146
currucipennella 534
cursoria 2083
curtula 2019
curvatula 1649
curvella 421
curvipunctosa 711
curvistrigana 934
cuspis 2282

Cyaniris 1578
Cybosia 2040
Cyclophora 1675
Cydia 1240
cydoniella 327
Cymatophorima 1658
Cynaede 1359
cynosbatella 1174
Cynthia 1591
cytisella 728

D

Dafa 643
dahlii 2121
DANAIDAE 1630
Danaus 1630
Daphnis 1985
daplidice 1552
Daraba 1412
Dasychira 2027
Dasypolia 2229
daucella 670

dealbana 1169
deauratella, Oegoconia 871
deauratella, Coleophora 519
debiliata 1861
decentella 20
deceptoria 2411
deciduana 1258
decimalis 2178
decolorella 874
decorata 1686
decorella 767
decrepitalis 1391
defoliaria 1935

degeerella 148
degenerana 2424
degeneraria 1714
degreyana 961
Deilephila 1991
Deileptenia 1940
delphinii 2398
Deltote 2413
demarniana 1135
demaryella 276
Dendrolimus 1639
denotata 1836
dentalis 1359
dentaria 1917
dentella, Phaulernis 477
dentella, Ypsolopha 453
denticulella 310
deplana 2049
depressana 683
Depressaria 669
DEPRESSARIINAE 666
depressella 683
depuncta 2013
deridens 2426
derivalis 2494
derivata 1747
desertella 786
designata 1722
desperatella 105
devoniella 304

dia 1602
Diachrysia 2433
Diacrisia 2059
diana 390
Diaphania 1409
Diaphora 2063
Diarsia 2120
Diasemia 1402
Diasemiopsis 1403
Dichonia 2247
Dichomeris 862
Dichrorampha 1273
Dicycla 2315
didyma 1611
didymata 1809
diffinis, Cosmia 2317
diffinis, Teleiopsis 776
Digitivalva 471
dilectella 407
Diloba 2020
dilucidana 949
diluta 1658
dilutaria 1704
dilutata 1795
dilutella 1462

dimidiata, Aglossa 1422
dimidiata, Idaea 1708
diminutalis 1351
diniana 1166
Dioryctria 1454
Diplodoma 180
dirce 1588
Discestra 2145
discipunctella 669
Discoloxia 1872
discordella 547
DISMORPHIINAE 1541
dispar, Lycaena 1562
dispar, Lymantria 2034
dispunctella 615
dissoluta 2371
distans 1491
distentella 346
distinctaria 1843
distinctata 1959
distinctella 791
distinguenda 113
ditella 211
ditrapezium 2127
Ditula 1010
Diurnea 663
diversana 982
dives 2210
divisella, Mompha 889
divisella, Monochroa 745

dodecella 760
dodonaea, Drymonia 2014
dodonaea, Tischeria 124
dodoneata 1853
dolabraria 1904
Dolicharthria 1399
domestica, Bryotropha 789
domestica, Cryphia 2293
dominula 2068
Donacaula 1330
dorsana 1252
dorylas 1577
doubledayana 1078
douglasella 677
douglassii 178
DOUGLASIIDAE 398

Drepana 1646
DREPANIDAE 1645
dromedarius 2000
drupiferarum 1977
drurella, Chrysoethia 746
drurella, Cosmopterix 896
druryella 896

Dryadaula 198
dryadella 56
Dryas 1583
Drymonia 2014
Dryobotodes 2248

dubiella 243
dubitana 964
dubitata 1790
dubitella 336
dulcella 52
dumerilii 2355
dumetana 973
duplana 1213
duplaris 1657

Dypterygia 2301
Dysauxes 2071
Dyscia 1969
Dysgonia 2460
dysodea 2165
Dystebenna 907

E

Eana 1028
Earias 2418

Ebulea 1385

Ecliptopera 1759
Ectocdemia 23
Ectomyelois 1460
Ectropis 1947

efformata 1868

egenaria 1824
Egira 2181

Eidophasia 469
Eilema 2043

ekebladella 123

Elachasta 593

ELACHISTIDAE 590
Elaphria 2396
electa 2453
Electrophaes 1773
eleochriella 628
Eligmodonta 2003
elinguaria 1921
elongella, Caloptilia 282
elongella, Monochroa 743
elpenor 1991
elutalis 1388
elutella 1473
elymi 2348

emargana 1062
emarginata 1712
Ematurga 1952
emberizaepenella 354
emeritella 679
Emmelia 2414
Emmelina 1524
emortualis 2495
empetrella 917
emutaria 1691

Enargia 2313
Enarmonia 1216
Endothenia 1097
Endotrichia 1424
ENDROMIDAE 1644
Endromis 1644
Endrosis 648
Enicostoma 668
enixalis 1346
ENNOMINAE 1884
Ennomos 1911
Entephria 1743

Epagoge 1006
Epermenia 481
EPERMENIIDAE 477
ephemeraeformis 194
Ephestia 1473
Epiblema 1174
Epichnopterix 189
Epichoristodes 997
epilobiella Roem. 880
epilobiella D. & S. 893
Epinotia 1130
Epione 1907
epiphron 1617
Epiphyas 998
Epirrhoe 1737
Epirrita 1795
Epischnia 1456

Epizeuxis. 2486
epomidion 2327
eppingella 188

equitella 393

Erannis 1935
Erebia 1617
eremita 2248
Eremobia 2352
ericella 1298
ericetana 1103
ericetella 797
ericinella 752
Eriocrania 6
ERIOCRANIIDAE 6
Eriogaster 1633
Eriopsela 1189
Eriopygodes 2175
erosaria 1915
erxlebella 447
Erynnis 1532
erythrocephala 2261
erythrogenella 32

Esperia 649

Etainia 20
Ethmia 717
ETHMIIDAE 717

Eublemma 2407
Eucalcia 2438
Eucarta 2310
Euchloe 1554
Euchoeca 1874
Euchromia 2072
EUCHROMIINAE 2072
Euchromius 1289
Euclemensia 901
Euclidia 2463
Eucosma 1190
Eucosmomorpha 1217
Eudemis 1113
Eudonia 1336
Eugnorisma 2103
Eugnosta 953
Eugraphe 2115
Euhyponomeuta 432
Eulamprotes 731
Eulia 1015
Eulithis 1754
Eumichtis 2255

euphorbiae, Acronicta 2288
euphorbiae, Hyles 1986
euphrosyne 1601
Euphyia 1793
Eupithecia 1811
Euplagia 2067
Euplexia 2305
EUPLOCAMINAE 197
Euplocamus 197
Eupoecilia 954
Euproctis 2029
Eupsilia 2256
eurema 49
Eurhodope 1438
Eurodryas 1610
Eurois 2137
Eurrhypara 1376
Eustroma 1772
Eustrotia 2412
Eutromula 389
Euxoa 2080
Euzophera 1469

Everes 1570
EVERGESTINAE 1356
Evergestis 1356
evonymella 424

Exaeretia 686
exanthemata 1956
Exapate 1026
exclamationis 2089
exigua 2385
exiguata 1819
Exoteleia 760
expallidata 1833
exsiccata 2296
exsoleta 2242
extensaria 1847
extersaria 1950
extimalis 1357
extrema 2347
exulis 2324
exultans 166

F

fabriciana 385
fagana 2422
fagaria 1969
fagata 1800
fagella 663
fagi, Hipparchia 1622

fagi, Stauropus 1999
fagiglandana 1259
fagivora 302
Fagivorina 1946
Falcaria 1645
falcataria 1648
falconipennella 289
fallacella 913
falsella 1316
Falseuncaria 960
fanfarae 1186
farinalis 1417
farinella 591
farreni 479
fascelina 2027
fasciana 1236
fasciapennella 433
fasciaria 1962
fasciella, Dichomeris 865
fasciella, Nemophora 144
fasciuncula 2340
favicolor 2200

Fedalmia 44
Feltia 2095
fenestratella 233
fennica 2100
ferchaultella 185
ferrago 2193
ferrugalis 1395
ferrugana 1044
ferrugata 1725
ferruginea 2302
ferruginella 229
festaliella 485
festucae 2439

fibulella 153
fictrix 247a
figulella 785
figulilella 1477
filicivora 200
filigrammaria 1798
filipendulae, Stigmella 57
filipendulae, Zygaena 169
fimbrialis 1672
fimbriata 2110
finitimella 308
firmata 1767
fixa 2395

flammatra 2101
flammea, Panolis 2179
flammea, Senta 2209

flammea, Trigonophora 2251
flammealis 1424
flammeolaria 1876
flavaginella 566
flavago 2364
flavalis 1396
flavescentella 244
flavicaput 904
flaviciliana 963
flavicincta 2252
flavicinctata 1743
flavicornis 1659
flavidorsana 1275
flavifrontella 661
flavimitrella 134
flavipennella 492
flavirena 2388
flaviventris 377
flavofasciata 1808
fletcherella 914
flexula 2473
floslactata 1693
floslactella 75
florida 2124
fluctuata 1728
fluctuosa 1656
fluxa 2349

foenella 1183
Fomoria 42
forficalis 1356
forficella 1329
formicaeformis 380
formosa 1445
formosana 1216
formosanus 1001
formosella 643
forsskaleana 1036
forsterana 1002
forsterella 394
Foveifera 1203

fragariella 51
francillana 950
frangulella 270
frater 2427
fraternana 1143
fraternella 830
fraxinata 1849
fraxinella 449
fraxini 2451
freyerella 631
friesei 445
frischella 517
froelichiella 358

fuciformis 1983
fucosa 2358
fugitivella 772
fuligana 1100
fuliginaria 2475
fuliginosa 2064
fulvalis 1359
fulvata 1765
fulvescens 893
fulviguttella 478
fulvimitrella 225
fumatella 790
funebrana 1247
funebris 1381
funerella 719
furcata 1777
furcatellus 1315
furcifera 2238
Furcula 1996
furcula 1997
furfurana 1110
furuncula 2341
furva 2329
fusca, Pyla 1451
fusca, Sterropteryx 195
fuscalis 1386
fuscantaria 1914
fuscatella 138
fuscescens 644
fuscicornis 520
fuscipunctella 237
fuscoanea 912
fuscocuprella 503
fuscolimbatus 1511
fusconebulosa 18
fuscovenosa 1705
fuscoviredella 396

G

galactodactyla 1514
galathea 1620
galbanella 784
galiata 1740
Galleria 1425
gallicana 1271
gallii 1987
gamma 2441
gangabella 620
Gastropacha 1642
gaunacella 126

gei 51
Gelechia 800

GELECHIIDAE 723
GELECHIINAE 723
geminana 1119
geminipuncta 2370
gemmella 755
gemmiferana 1244
geniculea 1309
geniculella 364
genistae 546
genitalana 1023
gentianaeana 1097
geoffrella 652
Geometra 1666
GEOMETRIDAE 1661
GEOMETRINAE 1664
germana 1237
gerningana 1008
gerronella 866
geryon 164

gi 51
Gibberifera 1173
gibbosella 859
gigantella 1328
gilvago 2275
gilvaria 1967
gilvicomana 933

glabratella 403
GLAPHYRIINAE 1360
glareosa 2117
glaucata 1651
glaucicolella 582
glaucinalis 1415
glaucinella 416
Glaucopsyche 1579
gleichenella 594
glitzella 507
globulariae 165
Gluphisia 2016
glutinosae 114
glyphica 2463
GLYPHIPTERIGIDAE 391
Glyphipterix 391
Glyphipteryx 902

gnaphalii 2218
gnidiella 1434
gnoma 2006
gnomana 1004
Gnophos 1963
Gnorimoschema 824

goedartella 411
Gonepteryx 1546
Goniodoma 488
gonodactyla 1501
goosensiata 1831
Gortyna 2364
gothica 2190

gracilis 2186
GRACILLARIIDAE 280
GRACILLARIINAE 280
graminis 2176
Grammodes 2461
grandaevana 1181
grandipennis 911
grandirena 2468
grandis 634
granella 215
granulatella 571
Graphania 2210
graphiphora 2114
graphodactyla 1505
griseata, Lithostege 1871
griseata, Timandra 1682
griseella 45
Griselda 1161
grisella 1426
griseola 2044
grossulariata 1884
grotiana 1006
gryphipennella 491

gueneana 1017
gueneeana 1284
gularis 1430

Gymnancyla 1464
Gymnoscelis 1862
Gypsonoma 1167
gysseleniella 442

H

Habrosyne 1653
Hada 2147
Hadena 2166
HADENINAE 2142
haidarabadi 250
halterata 1879
Halysidota 2066
hamana 937
Hamearis 1582

hamella 1299
hammoniella 157
Haplotinea 211
harpagula 1650
Harpyia 2004
harrisella 315
hartmanniana 941
hastana 1203
hastata 1787
hastiana 1053
haworthana 395
haworthi 11
haworthiata 1813
haworthii 2367

headleyella 44
hebenstreitella 983
Hecatera 2164
hecta 16
Hedya 1082
heegeriella 317
Heliodines 400
HELIODINIDAE 400
Heliophobus 2153
Heliothis 2400
Heliozela 154
HELIOZELIDAE 154
hellerella 905
Hellula 1360
helvola 2265
hemargyrella 81
Hemaris 1982
hemerobiella 523
hemidactylella 291
Hemistola 1673
Hemithea 1669
heparana 972
hepariella 435
hepatariella 685
hepatica 2149
HEPIALIDAE 14
Hepialus 14
heracliana, Agonopterix 688
heracliana, Depressaria 672
heringi 39
heringiana 1191
hermannella 746
herminata 180
Herminia 2488
Herpetogramma 1406
Hesperia 1529
HESPERIIDAE 1525
HESPERIINAE 1525
heterodactyla 1516
Heterogenea 174

hexadactyla 1288
heydeniana 957

HIEROXESTIDAE 277
Hipparchia 1621
hippocastanaria 1905
hippophaella 805
hippophaes 1989
hippothoe 1566
Hippotion 1993
hirtaria 1927
hispidaria 1925

Hofmanniella 312
Hofmannophila 647
hohenwartiana 1200
holmiana 1037
Homoeosoma 1480
Homona 975
Hoplodrina 2381
Horisme 1781
hornigi, Coleophora 509
hornigi, Monochroa 740
horridella 456
hortuella 1293
hortulata 1376
hostilis 1447

huebneri auct. 836
huebneri Haw. 837
humerella 842
humiliata 1706
humilis 606
humuli 14

hyale 1543
hyalinalis 1374
hybnerella 99
hybridella 965
Hydraecia 2361
Hydrelia 1876
Hydriomena 1777
hydrolapathella 500
hyemana 1055
Hylaea 1962
Hylephila 1530
Hyles 1986
Hyloicus 1978
Hymenia 1404
Hypagyrtis 1898
Hypanartia 1589
Hypatima 858
Hypena 2476

HYPENINAE 2476
Hypenodes 2485
hyperantus 1629
Hypercallia 657
Hypochalcia 1457
Hyppa 2320
Hypsopygia 1413
Hysterophora 924
Hysterosia 921

I

ibipennella 536

icarus 1574
icterata 1838
icteritia 2274
icterodactylus 1511

Idaea 1696
idaeella 505

ilicifolia 1641
illigerella 481
illuminatella 402
illunaris 2457

imbecilla 2175
imella 231
imitaria 1690
immorata 1683
immundana 1136
immundella 46
immutata 1692
imperialella 311
implicitana 956
impluviata 1778
impura 2198

Inachis 1597
incanana 1030
incarnatana 1179
incarnatella 468
incerta 2188
incertana 1024
incongruella 659
inconspicuella 177
Incurvaria 129
INCURVARIIDAE 128
INCURVARIINAE 128

indigata 1844
infida 1090
Infurcitinea 203
innotata 1848
inopiana 921
inornatella 867
inquilana 1227
inquinata 1703
inquinatana 1263
inquinatella 1306
insectella 212
insigniata 1820
insignitella 350
instabilella 812
insulana 2420
insularis 208
interjecta 2112
interjectana 1021
intermedialis 2483
internana 1242
interpunctella 1479
interrogationis 2447
intimella 25
intricata 1827
inturbata 1812
inulae 554

io 1597

Iphiclides 1540
Ipimorpha 2311
ipsilon 2091

iris 1585
irregularis 2168
irriguata 1818
irrorella, Setina 2036
irrorella, Yponomeuta 429

isabella 2065
Ischnoscia 205
isodactylus 1502
Isophrictis 729
Isotrias 1014
isterana 1165
Isturgia 1899

ivella 409

J

jacobaeae 2069
janiszewskae 910
janthina 2111
janthinana 1245

Jodia 2257
Jodis 1674
josephinae 660
jota 2443

jubata 1924
julia 1583
juncicolella 510
junctella 833
jungiella 1251
juniperata 1771
juniperella 863
Junonia 1586
junoniella 328
jurtina 1626
juventia 2308

K

Kessleria 433

kilmunella 598

kleemannella 360

knaggsiella 837

Kollariella 298

kroemanniella 836

kuehniella 1475

L

laburnella 254
Lacanobia 2156
lacertinaria 1645
Lacinipolia 2146
lactearia 1674
lacteella 887
lactucae 2215
lacunana 1076
Ladoga 1584
Laelia 2024
laetana 1123
laetus 1492
laevigata 1700
laevigatella 401
lafauryana 984
laisalis 1412
l-album 2202
lambdella 641
lamda 2239
Lampides 1567
Lampronia 131
Lampropteryx 1750
lancealana 1111
lancealis 1377
lanella 241
lanestris 1633
langiella 880
lantanella 331
Laothoe 1981
lapidata 1780
lapidella 184
lappella 724
lapponaria 1929
lapponica 116
Larentia 1745
LARENTIINAE 1717
laretella 222
laricella 526
lariciata 1856
laripennella 572
larseniella 844
Lasiocampa 1636
LASIOCAMPIDAE 1631
Lasiommata 1615
Laspeyria 2473
lassella 552
laterana 1038
lateritia 2328
lathamella 902
lathonia 1603
lathoniana 953
Lathronympha 1219
lathyrana 1250
lathyrifoliella 258

latifasciana 1038
latistria 1307
latreillei 2309
latreillella 900
latruncula 2339
lautella 351

leautieri 2240
lecheana 1000
legatella 1864
leguminata 1264
Leioptilus 1518
lemnata 1354
lentiginosella 793
leplastriana 1218
leporina 2280
Leptidea 1541
lethe, Euchromia 2072
lethe, Hypanartia 1589
leucapennella, Caloptilia 292
leucapennella, Coleophora 489
leucatella 758
Leucinodes 1411
Leucochlaena 2226
Leucodonta 2012
leucographa 2140
Leucoma 2031
leucophaearia 1932
Leucoptera 254
leucoschalis 1295
Leucospilapteryx 314
leucostigma 2368
leucostola 307
leucotreta 1215
leuwenhoekella 899
levana 1599
Levipalpus 685

libatrix 2469
lichenaria 1945
lichenea 2255
lichenella 179
Lichenovora 201
lienigialis 1416
lienigianus 1518
lienigiella 897
Ligdia 1888
ligea 1619
lignea 873
ligula 2259
ligustri, Craniophora 2291
ligustri, Sphinx 1976
limacodes 173
LIMACODIDAE 173
limbalis 1369

limbaria 1899
limbata 1900
limbella 918
limbirena 2430
limboundata 1695
Limnaecia 898
limoniella 488
limosipennella 499
linariata 1816
Lindera 210
lineana 1091
linearia 1681
lineata, Hyles 1990
lineata, Siona 1966
lineatella 857
lineola, Coleophora 522
lineola, Eudonia 1341
lineola, Thymelicus 1527
linetella 1319
linneella 903
lipsiana 1056
Lita 794
literana 1061
literosa 2342
Lithacodia 2410
lithargyrinella 524
LITHOCOLLETINAE 315
lithodactyla 1523
Lithomoia 2233
Lithophane 2235
Lithosia 2051
LITHOSIINAE 2035
Lithostege 1871
lithoxylea 2322
litoralis 2201
litterata 1402
littoralis, Lobesia 1109
littoralis, Spodoptera 2386
littorella 723
litura 2266
liturata 1893
liturella 698
liturosa 709
lixella 530

l-nigrum 2032

lobella 668
Lobesia 1105
Lobophora 1879
locupletella 882
loeflingiana 1032
loganella 300
logiana 1051
Lomaspilis 1887

Lomographa 1957
longana 1016
lonicerae 171
lophyrella 909
loreyi 2208
lorquiniana 1058
lota 2263
lotella, Anerstia 1432
lotella, Leucoptera 259
loti, 167
Lozotaenia 1002
Lozotaeniodes 1001

lubricalis 2487
lubricipeda 2060
lucella 457
lucens 2357
lucernalis 1409
lucernea 2104
lucida 2415
lucidella 736
lucina 1582
lucipara 2305
lucipeta 2106
lucteata 1786
luctuosa 2465
luculella 774
luedersiana 1224
Luffia 184
lunaedactyla 1495
lunalis 2490
lunana 1009
lunaris, Batia 640
lunaris, Minucia 2456
lunosa 2270
lunula 2223
lunulana 1252
lunularia 1918
Luperina 2353
Lupulinus 17
luridana 931
luridata 1734
lurideola 2050
lutarea, Metriotes 487
lutarea, Paraswammerdamia 441
lutatella 869
luteago 2169
luteella 112
luteolata 1906
luteum 2061
luticomella 600
lutipennella 490
lutosa 2375
lutulenta 2231
lutulentella 742
luzella 135

Lycaena 1561
LYCAENIDAE 1555
LYCAENINAE 1561
lychnidis 2267
lychnitis 2219
Lycia 1927
Lycophotia 2118
Lygephila 2466
Lymantria 2033
LYMANTRIIDAE 2024
Lyonetia 262
LYONETIIDAE 254
LYONETIINAE 262
Lysandra 1575
lythargyrella 1318
Lythria 1717

M

maccana 1060
Macdunnoughia 2436
machaon 1539
machinella 557
macilenta 2264
Macrochilo 2493
MACROGLOSSINAE 1982
Macroglossum 1984
Macrolythlacia 1638
maculana 1152
macularia 1909
Maculinea 1581
maculosana 924
maera 1616
maestingella 341
magdalenae 104
Malacosoma 1634
malella 97
malinellus 426
malvae 1534
malvella 809
Mamestra 2154
Manduca 1974
manihotalis 1418
Maniola 1626
manniana 926
mansuetella 2
Marasmarcha 1495
marcidella 475
margaritana 948
margaritata 1961
margaritella 1314
Margaritia 1368
margarotana 943
marginana 1099
marginaria 1934

marginata 1887
marginea 125
marginella 862
marginepunctata 1689
marginicolella 63
maritima, Bucculatrix 267
maritima, Eucosma 1195
maritima, Heliothis 2402
maritimella 585
maritimus 2391
marmorea 1440
marmoreum 829
Maruca 1401
masculella 130
matura 2303
maura 2300

Mecyna 1396
mediofasciella 35
mediopectinellus ·251
Meesia ·202
MEESSIINAE 201
megacephala 2278
Meganephria 2244
Meganola 2075
megera 1615
megerella 617
melagynalis 1347
melaleucanus 996
Melanargia 1620
Melanchra 2155
melanopa 2144
Melanthia 1784
Melissoblaptes 1429
Meliteae 1611
mellinata 1757
mellonella 1425
menciana 975
Mendesia 591
mendica, Argyresthia 417
mendica, Diaphora 2063
mendica, Diarsia 2120
Menophra 1936
menyanthidis 2286
mercurella 1344
mercuriana 1148
Mesapamea 2343
Mesogona 2141
Mesoleuca 1748
Mesoligia 2341
mesomella 2040
Mesophelps 860
Mesotype 1718
mespilella 325
messaniella 321
messingiella 469

metallica 147
metallicana 1072
metaxella 143
meticulosa 2306
metonella 242
Metriostola 1450
Metriotes 487
Metzneria 723
metzneriana 1196
metzneriella 726

mi 2462
miata 1761
micacea 2361
micella 734
microdactyla 1517
microgrammana 1220
MICROPTERIGIDAE 1
Micropterix 1
Microstega 1373
microtheriella 111
Microthrix 1449
Micrurapteryx 298
milhauseri 2004
millefoliata 1841
millenniana 1258
Miltochrista 2037
milvipennis 496
Mimas 1979
miniata 2037
minima 2345
minimana 927
minimella 145
minimus 1569
miniosa 2183
ministrana 1015
Minoa 1878
minorata 1805
minorella 393
Minucia 2456
minusculella 91
minutana 1171
minutella 645
Mirificarma 792
miscella 884
mitterbacheriana 1120

Mocis 2459
moeniacella Stt. 566
moeniacella auct. 574
moeniata 1729
moeschleri 2066
molesta 1248
Moma 2277
Mompha 880

MOMPHIDAE 878
MOMPHINAE 880
monacha 2033
monachella 232
moneta 2437
Monochroa 735
monodactyla 1524
monoglypha 2321
Monopis 227
monilifera 175
montanana 1283
montanata 1727
Mormo 2300
mormopis 235
morosa 137
morpheus 2387
Morphophaga 196
morrisii 2346
mouffetella 762
mucronata 1733
mucronella 451
mucronellus 1330
muelleriella 322
mulinella 792
multistrigaria 1775
munda 2189
mundana 2038
mundella 781
munitata 1723
muralis 2295
murana 1339
murariella 247b
muricata 1698
murinata 1878
murinella 821
muscaeformis 383
muscerda 2041
muscocella 803
musculana 986
musculosa 2378
musicola 2073
Mussidia 1466
mutatella 1455

Myelois 1458
mygindiana 1070
myllerana 388
myopaeformis 379
Myrmecozela 207
MYRMECOZELINAE 207
myrtillana, Ancylis 1128
myrtillana, Griselda 1162
myrtillella 72
myrtilli 2142
Mythimna 2191

N

Naenia 2136
naevana 1159
nana, Cochylis 968
nana, Hada 2147
nanana 1145
nanata 1846
nanatella 694
nanella 757
napi 1551
Narycia 175
Nascia 1387

nebulata 1874
nebulella 1480
nebulosa 2150
Nemapogon 215
NEMAPOGONINAE 211
Nematocampa 1900
Nematopogon 140
Nemaxera 223
NEMIOBIIDAE 1582
Nemophora 144
nemoralis, Agrotera 1410
nemoralis, Herminia 2492
nemorella, Crambus 1301
nemorella, Ypsolopha 452
nemorivaga 1141
Neofaculta 797
Neofriseria 798
Neosphaleroptera 1027
Nephopterix 1447
NEPTICULIDAE 19
nerii 1985
nervosa, Agonopterix 706
nervosa, Depressaria 670
neurica 2372
neuropterella 727
neustria 1634

ni 2432
nicaea 1988
nicellii 359
nickerlii 2354
Niditinea 237
nigra, Aporophyla 2232
nigra, Gelechia 806
nigrata 1366
nigrescentella 349
nigricana, Acleris 1140
nigricana, Cydia 1257
nigricans 2082
nigricomella 266

nigricostana 1102
nigripunctella 201
nigrivenella 1466
nigropunctata 1684
nimbella 1482
niobe 1605
nisella 1138
nitens 51
nitentella 815
nitidana 1222
nitidula 2417
nitidulana 1172
nivea 1331
niveicostella 548

Noctua 2107
noctualis 2409
noctuella 1398
NOCTUIDAE 2080
NOCTUINAE 2080
nodicolella 891
Nola 2077
NOLIDAE 2075
Nomophila 1398
Nonagria 2369
normalis 876
notana 1045
notata 1889
notatella 768
notha 1662
Nothris 838
Notodonta 2000
NOTODONTIDAE 1994

nubeculosa 2228
nubiferana 1083
nubigera 2404
nubilalis 1375
nubilana 1027
Nudaria 2038
nupta 2452

Nyctegretis 1468
Nycteola 2423
nylandriella auct. 104
nylandriella Tengst. 103
nymphaeata 1345
NYMPHALIDAE 1583
Nymphalis 1594
Nymphula 1345
NYMPHULINAE 1345

O

obelisca 2080
obeliscata 1768
obesalis 2479
obductella 1444
obfuscatus 1963
obliquella 70
oblitella 1467
obliteralis 1355
oblonga 2325
oblongana 1098
obscuralis 1349
obscurana 1225
obscuratus 1964
obscurepunctella 590
obseletana 1077
obsitalis 2478
obsoleta 2204
obsoletella 816
obstipata 1720
obtusa 2042
obtusana 1122
obumbratana 1202

occidentis 1105
occulta 2137
ocellalis 1423
ocellana, Agonopterix 701
ocellana, Spilonota 1205
ocellaris 2276
ocellata, Cosmorhoe 1752
ocellata, Smerinthus 1980
ocellatella 814
ocellea 1289
Ochlodes 1531
ochraceella, Mompha 886
ochraceella, Myrmecozela 207
ochrata 1696
ochrea 531
ochrearia 1968
ochrodactyla 1503
ochroleuca 2352
ochroleucana 1084
ochropacha 1657
Ochropleura 2099
Ochsenheimeria 251
ochsenheimeriana 1238
OCHSENHEIMERIIDAE 251
Ocnerostoma 444
ocnerostomella 398
ocularis 1654
oculea 2360

Odezia 1870
oditis 2226
ODONTIINAE 1359
Odontoptera 1920
Odontosia 2010

Oecophora 651
OECOPHORIDAE 634
OECOPHORINAE 634
Oegoconia 870
oehlmanniella 130
OENOCHROMINAE 1663
oenone 1587

Oidaematophorus 1523
OIKETICINAE 191
Oinophila 277

oleagina 2246
oleracea 2160
olerella 681
Olethreutes 1067
OLETHREUTINAE 1063
Oligia 2337
Oligostigma 1352
Olindia 1013
olivalis 1392
olivana 1075
olivata 1774
oliviella 650

omissella 314
Omphaloscelis 2270

Oncocera 1441
ononaria 1664
ononidis 299
onosmella 549

oo 2315

operculella 825
Operophtera 1799
OPHIDERINAE 2464
ophiogramma 2336
opima 2184
Opisthograptis 1906
Opogona 278
oporana 976

23

Opostega 119
OPOSTEGIDAE 119
oppressana 1170
Opsibotys 1386

or 1655
orana 999
orbitella 511
orbona 2108
Orgyia 2025
Oria 2378
orichalcea, Cosmopterix 896
orichalcea, Diachrysia 2433
orientalis 249
ornata 1687
ornatella 1463
ornitopus 2237
orobana 1253
orobi 257
orstadii 604
Orthonama 1719
Orthopygia 1415
Orthosia 2182
Orthotaelia 470
ORTHOTAELIINAE 470
Orthotaenia 1087

osseana 1029
osseatella 1471
osseella 750
osseola 2363
osthelderi 1311
osteodactylus 1520
ostrina 2407
ostrinalis 1363
Ostrinia 1375

otitae 551
otregiata 1751

Ourapteryx 1922

oxyacanthae, Allophyes 2245
oxyacanthae, Phyllonorycter
323
oxyacanthella 100
Oxyptilus 1489

P

pabulatricula 2332
Pachetra 2151
Pachycnemia 1905
Pachythelia 192
pactolana 1266
pactolia 198
padella 425
palaemon 1525
palaeno 1542
paleacea 2313
palealis 1370
paleana 989
pallens 2199
pallescentella 245
palliatella 537
pallida 1336
pallidactyla 1504
pallidana 967
pallidata 1358
pallidella 47
pallifrintana 1243
pallorella 700
pallustris 2392
palpella 653
palpina 2011
Palpita 1408
Paltodora 728
paludana 1127
paludella 1292
paludum 1493
palumbella 1442
palustrana 1074
palustrella 737
Pammene 1223
pamphilus 1627
Pancalia 899
pandalis 1373
Pandemis 969
pandora 1609
Panemeria 2397
Panolis 2179
pantaria 1886
PANTHEINAE 2425
panzerella 141
Papestra 2162
paphia 1608
Papilio 1539
papilionaria 1666
PAPILIONIDAE 1536
PAPILIONINAE 1539
pappiferella 570
Parachronistis 756
Paraclystola 656
Paracolax 2494

Paracorsia 1372
Paradiarsia 2116
paradoxa 82
paralellaria 1908
Paraleucoptera 261
Paralipsa 1430
Paramesia 1004
Paranthrene 372
PARANTHRENINAE 372
Parapoynx 1348
Pararge 1614
Parascotia 2475
Parasemia 2056
parasitella, Ephestia 1474
parasitella, Triaxomera 224
Parastichtis 2268
Paraswammerdamia 440
Parectopa 299
parenthesella 460
Pareulype 1785
pariana 389
paripennella 560
paripunctella 773
Parnalius 1538
PARNASSIINAE 1536
Parnassius 1536
Parocystola 656
Parornix 300
parthenias 1661
parva 2408
parvidactylus 1490
pascuella 1294
pasiuana 1022
pastinacella 672
pastinum 2466
paupella 748
pauperana 1198
pavonia 1643

pectinataria 1776
pectinea 129
pedella 877
Pediasia 1322
peliella 798
pellionella 240
Pelochrista 1188
Pelosia 2041
peltigera 2403
Pelurga 1749
Pempelia 1462
pendularia 1675
pennaria 1923
pentadactyla 1513
penthinana 1081
penziana 1031
percna 235

Perconia 1970
Peribatodes 1937
peribenanderi 559
peribolata 1730
Periclepsis 1005
Peridea 2005
Peridroma 2119
Perigia 2390
Periphanes 2398
Perittia 590
Perizoma 1801
perlella 1302
perlipedella 471
perlucidalis 1380
permixtana 928
permutana 1049
permutatella 1310
perplexa 2167
perpygmaeella 79
persicariae 2155
personella 218
petasitis 2362
petiverella 1273
Petrophora 1902
Petrova 1214
petryi 159
Pexicopia 809

pfeifferella 158

Phalera 1994
Phalonidia 926
phasianipennella 296
Phaulernis 477
phegea 2070
Pheosia 2006
Philedone 1008
Philedonides 1009
Philereme 1791
Philudoria 1640
phlaeas 1561
Phlogophora 2306
phoebus 1537
phoeniceata 1855
Photedes 2344
Phragmataecia 160
Phragmatobia 2064
phragmitella, Chilo 1290
phragmitella, Limnaecia 898
phragmitidis 2377
phryganella 664
Phtheochroa 925
Phthorimaea 825
phycidella 875

Phycita 1452
PHYCITINAE 1432
Phycitodes 1483
phyleus 1530
PHYLLOCNISTIDAE 367
Phyllocnistis 367
Phyllodesma 1641
Phyllonorycter 315
Phylloporia 128
Phytometra 2470

picaepennis 915
picarella 221
piceaella 759
pictalis 1419
piercei 942
piercella 238
PIERIDAE 1541
PIERINAE 1548
Pieris 1549
pigra 2017
pilella 142
pilleriana 1012
pilosaria 1926
pilosellae 1489
Pima 1453
pimpinellae 673
pimpinellata 1845
pinastri 1978
pinella 1313
pinguinalis 1421
pinguis 1470
pini 1639
piniaria 1954
piniariella 444
pinicolana 1211
pinicolella 879
pinivorana 1212
pirithous 1568
pisi 2163
pityocampa 2021

plagiata 1867
plagicolella 67
Plagodis 1903
plantaginis 2056
platanoidella 363
Plathypena 2481
Platyedra 808
platyptera 2224
Platyptilia 1499
PLATYPTILIINAE 1489
Platytes 1325
plebejana 1157
Plebejus 1571

Plebicula 1577
plecta 2102
Plemyria 1766
Pleuroptya 1405
Pleurota 654
plexippus 1630
Plodia 1479
plumbagana 1276
plumbana 1285
plumbella 430
plumbeolata 1814
plumella 189
plumigera 2013
Plusia 2439
PLUSIINAE 2428
Plutella 464
PLUTELLINAE 451

pneumonanthes 1505

poae 596
Poecilocampa 1631
podalirius 1540
podana 977
Polia 2148
poliellus 1308
politella 788
polychloros 1594
polychromella 850
Polychrysia 2437
polycommata 1880
polydectalis 1353a
Polygonia 1598
polygramata 1741
Polymixis 2252
polyodon 2097
Polyommatus 1574
Polyploca 1660
pomella 78
pomerana 605
pomiliella 248
pomonella, Cydia 1261
pomonella, Phyllonorycter 329
Pontia 1552
populana 1232
populata 1756
populella 853
populeti 2185
populetorum 281
populi, Laothoe 1981
populi, Poecilocampa 1631
porata 1679
porcellus 1992
porphyrana 1114
porphyrea 2118

porrectella 465
posticana 1208
postvittana 998
potatoria 1640
potentillae, Coleophora 513
potentillae, Scythris 920
poterii 59

praeangusta 878
praeatomata 1892
praecocella 404
praecox 2099
praeformata 1869
praelatella 132
prasina 2138
prasinana 2421
pratella 1300
pratellus 1301
Prays 449
prenanthis 2222
primaria 1960
Pristerognatha 1081
proboscidalis 2477
procellata 1784
procerella 639
processionea 2022
PROCRIDINAE 163
profulgella 480
profundana 1113
promissa 2454
pronuba 2107
pronubana 985
pronubella 446
propinquella, Agonopterix 696
propinquella, Mompha 888
prostratella 705
Protoschinia 2405
proximella 770
proximum 831
pruinata 1665
prunalis 1390
prunaria 1924
prunata 1754
prunetorum 109
pruni 1559
pruniana 1082
pruniella 420
prunifoliella 262
prunivorana 1249

Psamathocrita 750
Pselnophorus 1516
Pseudargyrotoza 1011
Pseudatemelia 660
Pseudenargia 2307

Pseudoips 2422
Pseudopanthera 1909
pseudospretella 647
Pseudosciaphila 1088
Pseudoswammerdamia 436
Pseudotephusa 764
Pseudoterpna 1665
psi 2284
psilella 823
Psodos 1965
Psoricoptera 859
Psyche 186
PSYCHIDAE 175
PSYCHINAE 183
Psychoides 199

Pterapherapteryx 1882
pterodactyla 1509
PTEROPHORIDAE 1487
PTEROPHORINAE 1510
Pterophorus 1510
Pterostoma 2011
Ptilodon 2008
Ptilodontella 2009
Ptilophora 2013
Ptocheuusa 748
Ptycholoma 1000
Ptycholomoides 987

pubicornis 139
pudibunda 2028
pudorina 2196
pulchella, Elachista 607
pulchella, Utetheisa 2054
pulchellana 974
pulchellata 1817
pulcherrimella 676
pulchrina 2442
Pulicalvaria 759
pulicariae 472
pulla 2234
pullana 1100
pulveralis 1383
pulveraria 1903
pulveratella 754
pulverella 703
pulverosella 40
punctalis, Dolicharthria 1399
punctalis, Synaphe 1414
punctaria 1680
punctidactyla 1498
punctinalis 1944
punctosa 387
punctulata 1951
pupillana 1199
puppillaria 1678

resinella, Petrova 1214
resplendella 156
reticulata 2153
reticulatum 1772
retiella 190
retinella 415
retusa 2311
Reuttia 840
revayana 2423
revinctella 622

rhamni 1546
rhamniella 908
rhediella 1239
Rheumaptera 1787
Rhigognostis 466
Rhizedra 2375
rhododactyla 1496
Rhodometra 1716
rhombana 1042
rhombella 800
rhomboidaria 1937
rhomboidea 2131
rhomboidella 858
Rhopobota 1158
Rhyacia 2105
Rhyacionia 1210
Rhynchopacha 761

ribeata 1940
richardsoni 202
ridens 1660
ripae 2093
rivata 1739
Rivula 2474
rivulana 1068
rivularis 2166
rivulosa 2406

roborana 1178
roboraria 1943
roborella, Phycita 1452
roborella, Stigmella 86
roboris 316
robustana 1112
robustella 287
roesella 400
Roeslerstammia 446
rorrella 428
rosaceana 1064
rosaecolana 1177
rosana 981
roseana 962
rostralis 2480

rotundella 716

ruberata 1779
rubi, Callophrys 1555
rubi, Diarsia 2123
rubi, Macrothylacia 1638
rubidata 1735
rubiella 136
rubigana 946
rubiginata, Plemyria 1766
rubiginata, Scopula 1688
rubiginea 2260
rubiginosana 1146
rubivora 31
rubricollis 2039
rubricosa 2139
rufa 2379
rufana, Acleris 1057
rufana, Celypha 1065
rufata 1865
rufescens 868
ruficapitella 84
ruficiliana 960
ruficornis 2015
rufifasciata 1862
rufimitrana 1164
rufimitrella 152
rufipennella 284
rufocinerea 608
rugosana 925
rumicis 2289
rumina 1538
rupicapraria 1960
rupicola 959
ruralis 1405
ruricolella 219
rurinana 992
Rusina 2302
rusticella 227
rutella 209
rutilana 940

S

sabella 1431
sabinella 802
Sabre 1650
sabulifera 2471
sacchari 278
sacraria 1716
sagitella 366
sagittata 1810
sagittigera 2151
salaciella 119
Salagia 1448

Salebriopsis 1446
salicalis 2472
salicata 1753
salicella, Cheimophila 665
salicella, Hedya 1086
salicicolella 335
salicis, Leucoma 2031
salicis, Stigmella 68
salicorniae 588
saligna 367
salinella, Coleophora 575
salinella, Scrobipalpa 813
salmachus 373
salopiella 10
samadensis 811
sambucaria 1922
samiatella 88
sangiella 845
sangii 12
sanguinalis 1364
sannio 2059
saportella 319
sarcitrella 648
SARROTHRIPINAE 2423
satura 2249
saturatella 545
Saturnia 1643
SATURNIIDAE 1643
satyrata 1828
SATYRIDAE 1614
saucia 2119
sauciana 1096
saxicola 1484
saxifragae, Kessleria 434
saxifragae, Stenoptila 1506

scabiosella, Nemophora 147
scabiosella, Phyllonorycter 355
scabra 2481
scabrella 455
scabriuscula 2301
scalella 764
SCARDIINAE 196
schalleriana 1047
Schiffermuelleria 634
Schinia 2406
schistacea 1560
schmidiella 895
schmidtiellus 861
schoenicolella 392
Schoenobius 1328
Schrankia 2482
schreberella 352
Schreckensteinia 485
SCHRECKENSTEINIIDAE 485

schreiberiana 922
schulziana 1073
schumacherana 1013
schwarziellus 141
scirpi 627
scitella 260
scoliaeformis 376
Scoliopteryx 2469
scolopacina 2335
Scoparia 1332
scopariella, Agonopterix 704
scopariella, Phyllonorycter 340
SCOPARIINAE 1332
scopigera 382
Scopula 1683
scoticella 305
scotinella 801
Scotochrosta 2234
Scotopteryx 1729
scriptella 766
Scrobipalpa 810
Scrobipalpula 823
scrophulariae 2220
scutosa 2405
scutulana 1184
SCYTHRIDIDAE 911
Scythris 911
Scythropia 450

secalis 2343
sedatana 1286
Sedina 2376
segetum 2087
sehestediana 387
Selania 1218
selasella 1303
selene 1600
Selenia 1917
Selidosema 1938
semele 1621
semiargus 1578
semibrunnea 2235
semicostella 841
semifascia 290
semifasciana 1089
semifulvella 246
semifusca 419
Semioscopis 666
Semiothisa 1889
semipurpurella 13
semirubella 1441
semitestacella 423
senecionana 991
senectana 1277
senectella 782
senex 2035

senilella 466
Senta 2209
sepium 183
septembrella 42
sequana 1278
sequax 775
sequella 462
serella 61
seriata 1707
sericea 2048
sericealis 2474
sericiella 154
sericopeza 21
serpentata 1697
serpylletorum 542
Serraca 1944
serratella 493
serricornis 626
servillana 1256
Sesia 370
SESIIDAE 370
SESIINAE 370
Setina 2036
Setomorpha 209
SETOMORPHINAE 209
sexalata 1882
sexguttella 747
sexstrigata 2133
sexta 1975

shepherdana 1046

siccella 916
slccIfulia 501
Sideridis 2152
signaria 1891
signatana 1144
signatella 872
silaceata 1759
silacella 860
silenella 550
silesiaca 684
silvella 1296
similella, Microthrix 1449
similella, Schiffermuelleria 636
similis, Bryotropha 780
similis, Euproctis 2030
simplana 1173
simpliciana 1281
simpliciata 1842
simpliciella 391
simulans 2105
Simyra 2290
sinapis 1541
singula 799

sinuella, Homoeosoma 1481
sinuella, Paraleucoptera 261
Siona 1966
siterata 1760
Sitochroa 1370
Sitotroga 749

smaragdaria 1668
smeathmanniana 947
Smerinthus 1980

sobrina 2116
socia 2236
sociana 1168
sociella 1428
sodaliana 923
solandriana 1156
Solenobia 176
SOLENOBIINAE 175
solidaginis 2233
solitariella 525
solutella 795
somnulentella 264
Sophronia 841
sorbi, Phyllonorycter 324
sorbi, Stigmella 66
sorbiella 413
sordens 2334
sordiana 1153
Sorhagenia 908
sororcula 2043
sororculana 1095
sororcullella 802a
sororiata 1866

spadicearia 1724
Spaelotis 2113
sparganella 470
Spargania 1786
sparganii 2373
Sparganothis 1012
sparrmannella 9
sparsana 1041
sparsata 1863
sparshalli 2023
spartiella 856
spartifoliella 256
Spatalistis 1034
spatulella 122
speciosa 65
spectrana 993
specularis 1312
spheciformis 375
sphendamni 22

SPHINGIDAE 1971
SPHINGINAE 1971
Sphinx 1976
sphinx 2227
spilodactylus 1515
Spilonota 1205
Spilosoma 2060
spiniana 1231
spiniella 440
spinifera 2086
spinolella 337
spinosella 27
spinosissimae 94
Spiris 2052
spissicornis 518
splendana 1260
splendidissimella 53
splendidulana 1223
Spodoptera 2385
sponsa 2455
Spuleria 904

squamosella 569

stabilella 633
stabilis 2187
stachydalis 1384
stagnana 1161
stagnata 1350
Standfussiana 2104
staneela 155
stannella 432
Stathmopoda 877
STATHMOPODIDAE 877
statices 163
staticis 1487
Stauropus 1999
steinkellneriana 667
stellatarum 1984
Stenodes 935
Stenolechia 755
Stenoptilia 1505
stephensi 907
Stephensia 592
stephensiana 1020
sternipennella 566
STERRHINAE 1675
Sterropterix 195
stettinensis 357
sticticalis 1368
stigmatella 288
Stigmella 50
Stilbia 2394
stolida 2461
straminata 1715

straminea, Mythimna 2197
straminea, Stenodes 936
straminella 1304
strataria 1930
stratiotata 1348
streliciella 824
striana 1063
striata 2052
striatella 729
striatipennella 553
strigana 1219
strigilata 2488
strigilis 2337
strigillaria 1970
strigosa 2285
strigula 2075
strigulatella 344
strobilella 1254
stroemiana 1151
Strophedra 1221
Strymonidia 1558

suadella 810
suaedivora 574
suasa 2159
suavella 1438
subalbidella 621
subaquilea 635
subbimaculella 38
subbistrigella 892
subcinerea 808
subdecurtella 751
subdivisella 890
suberivora 85
subfasciella 443
subfusca 1332
subfuscata 1837
subgothica 2095
sublustris 2323
subnigrella 603
subocellana, Epinotia 1132
subocellana, Lozotaenia 1003
subocellea, Elachista 613
subocellea, Reuttia 840
subochreella 661
subpropinquella 692
subpurpurella 6
subrosea 2115
subroseana 958
subsequana, Acrolita 1160
subsequana, Epinotia 1130
subsericeata 1709
subterranea 2096
subtusa 2312
subumbrata 1840
succedana 1255

succenturiata 1839
suffamata 1750
suffusella 741
sulphurella 649
superstes 2383
suspecta 2268
suspectana 1230

svenssoni 87

swammerdamella 140
Swammerdamia 437

sylvata, Abraxas 1885
sylvata, Hydrelia 1877
sylvaticella 580
sylvella, Phyllonorycter 362
sylvella, Ypsolopha 459
sylvestrana 1206
sylvestraria 1701
sylvestris 1526
sylvicolana 1282
sylvina 15
Symmoca 872
SYMMOCINAE 870
Synanthedon 373
Synaphe 1414
Synclita 1355
Syncopacma 844
Syndemis 986
Synedoida 2468
SYNGRAPHA 2447
Syntarucus 1568
Synthymia 2395
SYNTOMINAE 2070
Syntomis 2070
syringaria 1910
syringella 293

T

tabaniformis 372
taenialis 2482
taeniatum 1801
taeniipennella 581
taeniolella 847
tages 1532
Taleporia 181
TALEPORIINAE 180
tamarisciata 1850
tamesis 583
tantillaria 1857
tapetzella 234

tarsicrinalis 2491
tarsipennalis 2489
Tathorhynchus 2296

Tebenna 386
tedella 1142
TEICHOBIINAE 199
Telechrysis 646
Teleiodes 765
Teleiopsis 776
Telephila 861
temerata 1958
temerella 852
templi 2229
Tenaga 248
tenebrata 2397
tenebrella 735
tenebrosana 1246
tenerana 1139
tenerella 318
tengstroemi 60
tentaculella 1327
tenuiata 1811
tephradactyla 1522
Tephronia 1953
terebrella 1461
terminella, Ethmia 717
terminella, Mompha 881
ternata 1694
terrealis 1379
terrella 787
tersata 1782
tessellatella 210
tesseradactyla 1499
tesserana 939
testacea 2353
testata 1755
testulalis 1401
Tethea 1654
Tetheella 1656
tetragonana 1180
tetragonella 738
tetralunaria 1919
tetrapunctella 761
tetraquetrana 1137

thalassina 2158
Thalera 1672
Thalpophila 2303
Thaumetopoea 2021
THAUMETOPOEIDAE 2021
Thecla 1556
THECLINAE 1555
Thera 1767
Theria 1960

tumidella 1436
tunbergella 1
turbidana, Apotomis 1092
turbidana, Epiblema 1182
turbidella 24
turca 2191
turfosalis 2485
turicensis 243
turionella 1209
turpella 807

typhae 2369
typica 2136
Tyria 2069
Tyta 2465

U

uddmanniana 1175
Udea 1388

ulicetella 705
ulicicolella 339
ulicis 2307
uliginosalis 1393
uliginosellus 1297
ulmariae 58
ulmella, Bucculatrix 274
ulmella, Scoparia 1335
ulmifoliella 353
ulmiphaga 96
ulmivora 80
ulmltella 671

umbra 2399
umbrana 1052
umbratica 2216
umbrosella 778

unangulata 1794
unanimis 2331
uncella 1118
uncula 2412
unculana 1125
undalis 1360
undulana 1087
undulata 1789
unguicella 1117
unicolor 193
unicolorella 732
unifasciella 619

unimaculella 8
unionalis 1408
unipuncta 2203
unipunctana 1159
unipunctata 1898
unipunctella 368
unitana 990
unitella 642

upupana 1121

Uresiphita 1369
urticae, Aglais 1593
urticae, Spilosoma 2062

ustatella 864
ustella 461
ustomaculana 1158
ustulana 1101

Utetheisa 2054
utonella 629

V

vaccinii 2258
vacculella 253
vagans 1411
Valeria 2246
valerianata 1821
vandaliella 1343
Vanessa 1590
variabilis 2438
variata 1769
variegana 1048
variella 917
v-ata 1858

vectisana 929
velocella 796
venata 1531
venosata 1823
Venusia 1873
venustula 2396
verbascalis 1382
verbascella 838
verbasci 2221
verellus 1317
verhuella 199
versicolor 2338

W

X

Y

YPONOMEUTINAE   424
ypsillon   2314
Ypsolopha   451

Z

Zeiraphera   1163
zelleri   1429
Zelleria   435
ZERYNTHIINAE   1538
Zeuzera   161
ZEUZERINAE   160

ziczac   2003
zieglerella   894
zinckenii   129

zoegana   938
zollikoferi   2356
zonaria   1928
zophodactylus   1507
Zophodia   1464a

Zygaena   166
ZYGAENIDAE   163
ZYGAENINAE   166

From addenda and corrigenda

adjectella   496a
aegopodiella   680
aprilella   727a
arcuatella, Archinemapogon   222
Athrips   761
atomella   703
autumnitella   476

bifasciella   871a
bonnetella   421
britannica   1769

Calliteara   2028
caradjai   871a
catoptrana   1191
Choreutis   389
Cochylimorpha   935
convolutella   1464a
crisonalis   1351b

Dasystoma   664
delunella   1343
deviella   574
Dicallomera   2027

fluctuosalis   1351a
fuscella   237

gardesanella   557
grossulariella   1464a

haasi   465a
Heliothis   2400
heydeni   216a
hyalinata   1409

inconditella   2169
inspersella   920a

lacustrata   1338
laterella   222
lathoniellus   1301
linosyridella   556a
littoricola   616a
lutealis   1388

malifoliella   260
manilensis   1347a
maritima, Phycitodes   1485

nanivora   437a

obscurella   607
obviella   229
occultella   34

Paradarisa   1949
passerella   437a
Phibalapteryx   1718
Prochoreutis   387

Retina   1214

Sabra   1650
saxicolella   565
Sceliodes   1412
schuetzeella   1454a
secundaria   1937a
stagnalis   1351b

torridana   1203
Trachysmia   922
trifasciata, Argyresthia   409a
trigonella   1151

ENGLISH NAMES

A

Adonis Blue   1576

African   2390
African Carnation Tortrix
  997

Albin's Hampstead Eye   1586
Alchymist   2464
Alder Kitten   1996
Alder Moth   2281

American Painted Lady   1592

Angle Shades   2306
Angle-barred Pug   1848
Angle-striped Sallow   2313
Angoumois Grain Moth   749
Annulet   1964
Anomalous   2394
Antirrhinum Brocade   2224
Antler Moth   2176

Aphrodite Fritillary   1604
Apollo   1536
Apple & Plum Case Bearer
  495
Apple Ermine   246
Apple Fruit Moth   418
Apple Leaf Miner   263
Apple Leaf Skeletonizer   389
Apple Pith Moth   906
Apple Pygmy   97

Archer's Dart   2085
Argent & Sable   1787
Arran Brown   1619
Arran Carpet   1763

Ash Bud Moth   449
Ash Pug   1849
Ash Shoulder-knot   2234
Ashworth's Rustic   2129

August Thorn   1912
Autumn Green Carpet   1761
Autumnal Moth   1797

Autumnal Rustic   2117
Autumnal Snout   2483

Azalea Leaf Miner   285

B

Balsam Carpet   1721
Barberry Carpet   1785
Barred Carpet   1801
Barred Chestnut   2121
Barred Fruit-tree Tortrix   970
Barred Hook-tip   1647
Barred Red   1962
Barred Rivulet   1804
Barred Sallow   2272
Barred Straw   1758
Barred Tooth-striped   1880
Barred Umber   1903
Barred Yellow   1765
Barret's Marbled Coronet   2169
Basker   2072
Bath White   1552

Beaded Chestnut   2267
Beautiful Arches   2249
Beautiful Brocade   2156
Beautiful Carpet   1748
Beautiful China-mark   1350
Beautiful Golden Y   2442
Beautiful Gothic   2226
Beautiful Hook-tip   2473
Beautiful Snout   2476
Beautiful Utetheisa   2055
Beautiful Yellow Underwing
  2142
Bedstraw Hawk-moth   1987
Bee Moth   1428
Beech-green Carpet   1774
Beet Moth   814
Belted Beauty   1928
Berber   2307
Berger's Clouded Yellow   1544

Bilberry Pug   1861
Bilberry Tortrix   988
Birch Mocha   1677
Bird-cherry Ermine   424
Bird's Wing   2301

Black Arches   2033

Black Collar   2101
Black Hairstreak   1559
Black Mountain Moth   1965
Black Rustic   2232
Black Snout   2481
Black V Moth   2032
Black-banded   2253
Blackberry Looper   1671
Blackneck   2466
Black-veined Moth   1966
Black-veined White   1548
Blair's Mocha   1678
Blair's Shoulderknot   2240
Blair's Wainscot   2376
Bleached Pug   1833
Blomer's Rivulet   1872
Blood Vein   1682
Blossom Underwing   2183
Blotched Emerald   1667
Bloxworth Snout   2478
Blue Pansy   1587
Blue-bordered Carpet   1766

Bond's Wainscot   2346
Bordered Beauty   1907
Bordered Chequer   1900
Bordered Gothic   2153
Bordered Grey   1938
Bordered Pearl   1373
Bordered Pug   1839
Bordered Sallow   2399
Bordered Straw   2403
Bordered White   1954

Bramble Shoot Moth   1175
Brick   2262
Bright Wave   1696
Bright-line Brown-eye   2160
Brighton Wainscot   2378
Brimstone   1546
Brimstone Moth   1906
Brindled Beauty   1927
Brindled Green   2248
Brindled Ochre   2229
Brindled Pug   1852
Brindled White-spot   1950
Brixton Beauty   2417
Broad-barred White   2164
Broad-bordered Bee
    Hawk-moth   1983
Broad-bordered White
    Underwing   2144
Broad-bordered Yellow
    Underwing   2110
Broken-barred Carpet   1773

Broom Moth   2163
Broom-tip   1865
Brother   2427
Brown Argus   1572
Brown China-mark   1345
Brown House-moth   647
Brown Oak Tortrix   979
Brown Rustic   2302
Brown Scallop   1791
Brown Silver-line   1902
Brown-line Bright-eye   2192
Brown-spot Pinion   2266
Brown-tail   2029
Brown-veined Wainscot   2371
Brussels Lace   1945

Bud Moth   1205
Buff Arches   1653
Buff Ermine   2061
Buff Footman   2049
Buff-tip   1994
Bulrush Wainscot   2369
Burnet Companion   2463
Burnished Brass   2434
Burren Green   2366
Butterbur   2362
Buttoned Snout   2480

C

Cabbage Moth   2154
Cacao Moth   1473
Camberwell Beauty   1596
Camellia Tortrix   975
Campanula Pug   1836
Campion   2166
Canary-shouldered Thorn   1913
Carnation Tortrix   985
Case-bearing Clothes Moth   240

Centre-barred Sallow   2269

Chalk Carpet   1731
Chalk Hill Blue   1575
Chamomile Shark   2214
Chequered Fruit-tree Tortrix
    969
Chequered Skipper   1525
Cherry Fruit Moth   420
Cherry-bark Moth   1216
Chestnut   2258
Chestnut-coloured Carpet   1770
Chevron   1755
Chimney Sweeper   1870

Chinese Character 1651
Chocolate Tip 2019

Cinnabar 2069
Cistus Forester 164

Clay 2193
Clay Fan-foot 2494
Clay Triple-lines 1681
Cleopatra 1547
Clifden Nonpareil 2451
Cloaked Carpet 1793
Cloaked Minor 2341
Cloaked Pug 1815
Clouded August Thorn 1916
Clouded Border 1887
Clouded Brindle 2327
Clouded Buff 2059
Clouded Drab 2188
Clouded Magpie 1885
Clouded Silver 1958
Clouded Yellow 1545
Clouded-bordered Brindle
    2326

Coast Dart 2083
Cocksfoot Moth 391
Codling Moth 1261
Comma 1598
Common Blue 1574
Common Carpet 1738
Common Clothes Moth 236
Common Emerald 1669
Common Fan-foot 2488
Common Footman 2050
Common Heath 1952
Common Lutestring 1657
Common Marbled Carpet 1764
Common Pug 1834
Common Quaker 2187
Common Rustic 2343
Common Swift 17
Common Wainscot 2199
Common Wave 1956
Common White Wave 1955
Concolorous 2347
Conformist 2238
Confused 2329
Convolvulus Hawk-moth 1972
Copper Underwing 2297
Cork Moth 216
Corn Moth 215
Coronet 2291
Cosmopolitan 2208

Cousin German 2116
Coxcomb Prominent 2008

Cream-bordered Green Pea
    2418
Cream-spot Tiger 2058
Crescent 2368
Crescent Dart 2090
Crescent Striped 2325
Crimson Speckled 2054
Crinan Ear 2359

Cudweed 2218
Cumberland Gem 2310
Cumbrian Umber 1783
Currant Clearwing 373
Currant Pug 1832
Currant Shoot Borer 133

Cyclamen Tortrix 993
Cypress Pug 1855

D

Dappled White 1554
Dark Arches 2321
Dark Bordered Beauty 1908
Dark Brocade 2250
Dark Chestnut 2259
Dark Crimson Underwing
    2455
Dark Dagger 2283
Dark Fruit-tree Tortrix 972
Dark Green Fritillary 1607
Dark Marbled Carpet 1762
Dark Spectacle 2449
Dark Spinach 1749
Dark Sword-grass 2091
Dark Tussock 2027
Dark Umber 1792
Dark-barred Twin-spot
    Carpet 1725

Death's-head Hawk-moth 1973
December Moth 1631
Deep-brown Dart 2231
Delicate 2195
Dentated Pug 1863
Devon Carpet 1751
Devonshire Wainscot 2206
Dew Moth 2035

Dewick's Plusia   2436

Diamond-back Moth   464
Dingy Angle   1892
Dingy Footman   2044
Dingy Mocha   1675
Dingy Shears   2314
Dingy Shell   1874
Dingy Skipper   1532

Docker   2074
Dog's Tooth   2159
Dot Moth   2155
Dotted Border   1934
Dotted Border Wave   1701
Dotted Carpet   1942
Dotted Chestnut   2260
Dotted Clay   2130
Dotted Fan-foot   2493
Dotted Footman   2041
Dotted Rustic   2105
Double Dart   2114
Double Kidney   2311
Double Line   2191
Double Lobed   2336
Double Square-spot   2128
Double-barred   2458
Double-spot Brocade   2244
Double-spotted Spangle   2446
Double-striped Pug   1862

Drab Looper   1878
Dried Currant Moth   1476
Dried Fruit Moth   1478
Drinker   1640

Duke of Burgundy Fritillary
   1582
Dumeril's Rustic   2355
Dun-bar   2318
Dungeness Pygmy Footman
   2046
Dusky Brocade   2330
Dusky Carpet   1953
Dusky Clearwing   372
Dusky Hook-tip   1649
Dusky Marbled Brown   2016
Dusky Sallow   2352
Dusky Thorn   1914
Dusky-lemon Sallow   2275

Dwarf Cream Wave   1705
Dwarf Pug   1857

E

Ear Moth   2360
Early Grey   2243
Early Moth   1960
Early Thorn   1917
Early Tooth-striped   1881
Eastern Bordered Straw   2404

Edinburgh Pug   1827

Egyptian Bollworm   2420

Elephant Hawk-moth   1991
Elgin Shoot Moth   1213

Emperor Moth   1643

Engrailed   1947

Essex Emerald   1668
Essex Skipper   1527

European Corn-borer   1375
European Map   1599
European Vine Moth   1107

Eversmann's Rustic   2100

Exile   2324

Eyed Hawk-moth   1980

F

False Codling Moth   1215
False Grayling   1624
False Mocha   1679
False Water Betony   2222
Fan-foot   2489

Feathered Brindle   2230
Feathered Ear   2151
Feathered Footman   2052
Feathered Gothic   2178
Feathered Ranunculus   2255
Feathered Thorn   1923
Fen Square-spot   2124
Fen Wainscot   2377
Fenn's Wainscot   2351
Fern   1782
Festoon   173

Fiery Clearwing   384
Fiery Skipper   1530
Figure of Eight   2020
Figure of Eighty   1654
Fisher's Estuarine Moth   2365
Five-spot Burnet   170
Five-spotted Hawk-moth   1974

Flame   2098
Flame Brocade   2251
Flame Carpet   1722
Flame Shoulder   2102
Flame Wainscot   2209
Flax Tortrix   1021
Flounced Chestnut   2265
Flounced Rustic   2353

Forester   163
Fortified Carpet   1729
Four-dotted Footman   2040
Four-spotted   2465
Four-spotted Footman   2051
Fox   1638
Foxglove Pug   1817

Freyer's Pug   1827
Frosted Green   1660
Frosted Orange   2364
Frosted Yellow   1899
Fruitlet Mining Tortrix   1239

G

Galium Carpet   1740
Garden Carpet   1728
Garden Dart   2082
Garden Pebble   1356
Garden Rose Tortrix   1048
Garden Tiger   2057

Gatekeeper   1625

Gem   1720
Geometrician   2461

Ghost Moth   14

Glanville Fritillary   1612
Glaucous Shears   2162

Goat Moth   162
Gold Spangle   2444
Gold Spot   2439
Gold Swift   16
Gold Triangle   1413
Golden Plusia   2437
Golden Twin-spot   2428
Golden-rod Brindle   2233
Golden-rod Pug   1851
Goldwing   2395
Gothic   2136
Gothic Dart   2095

Grass Eggar   1636
Grass Emerald   1665
Grass Rivulet   1807
Grass Wave   1970
Grayling   1621
Great Dart   2094
Great Kidney   2468
Great Oak Beauty   1943
Great Prominent   2005
Green Arches   2138
Green Carpet   1776
Green Hairstreak   1555
Green Oak Tortrix   1033
Green Pug   1860
Green Silver-lines   2422
Green Silver-spangled Shark
   2212
Green-brindled Crescent   2245
Green-brindled Dot   2246
Green-underside Blue   1578
Green-veined White   1551
Gregson's Dart   2086
Grey   2174
Grey Arches   2150
Grey Birch   1951
Grey Carpet   1871
Grey Chi   2254
Grey Dagger   2284
Grey Mountain Carpet   1744

Grey Pine Carpet   1768
Grey Pug   1837
Grey Scalloped Bar   1969
Grey Shoulder-knot   2237
Grey Tortrix   1020
Grizzled Skipper   1534
Ground Lackey   1635

Gypsy Moth   2034

H

Handmaid   2071
Haworth's Minor   2367
Haworth's Pug   1813
Hawthorn Moth   450

Heart & Club   2088
Heart & Dart   2089
Heart Moth   2315
Heath Fritillary   1613
Heath Rivulet   1805
Heath Rustic   2135
Hebrew Character   2190
Hedge Brown   1625
Hedge Rustic   2177
Herald   2469
Hermit   1623

High Brown Fritillary   1606

Hoary Footman   2045
Holly Blue   1580
Holly Tortrix   1159
Hollyhock Seed Moth   809
Honeysuckle Moth   453
Hornet Moth   370
Horse Chestnut   1905

Humming-bird Hawk-moth   1984

I

Indian Meal Moth   1479
Ingrailed Clay   2120

Iron Prominent   2000

Isabelline Tiger   2065
Isle of Wight Wave   1706

J

Jasione Pug   1836

Jersey Tiger   2067

Julia   1583
July Belle   1734
July Highflyer   1777
Juniper Carpet   1771
Juniper Pug   1854
Juniper Webber   862

K

Kent Black Arches   2076
Kentish Glory   1644
Kew Arches   2180

Kidney-spotted Minor   2146

Knot Grass   2289

L

Laburnum Leaf Miner   254
Lace Border   1687
Lackey   1634
L-album Wainscot   2202
Lang's Short-tailed Blue   1568
Lappet   1642
Larch Case-bearer   526
Larch Pug   1856
Larch Tortrix   1166
Large Blue   1581
Large Clover Case-bearer   516
Large Copper   1562
Large Dagger   2282
Large Dark Prominent   2001
Large Ear   2357
Large Emerald   1666
Large Fruit-tree Tortrix   977
Large Heath   1628
Large Lace Border   1695

Large Nutmeg   2333
Large Pale Clothes Moth   245
Large Ranunculus   2252
Large Red-belted Clearwing
   381
Large Skipper   1531
Large Tabby   1421
Large Thorn   1911
Large Tortoiseshell   1594
Large Twin-spot Carpet   1726
Large Wainscot   2375
Large Wall   1616
Large White
Large Yellow Underwing   2107
Latin   2308
Latticed Heath   1894

Lead Belle   1733
Lead-coloured Drab   2185
Lead-coloured Pug   1814
Least Black Arches   2078
Least Carpet   1699
Least Minor   2344
Least Yellow Underwing   2112
Leek Moth   473
Lempke's Gold Spot   2440
Leopard Moth   161
Lesser Belle   2472
Lesser Broad-bordered Yellow
   Underwing   2111
Lesser Cream Wave   1692
Lesser Lichen Case-bearer   177
Lesser Swallow Prominent   2006
Lesser Treble-bar   1868
Lesser Wax Moth   1426
Lesser Yellow Underwing   2109
Lesser-spotted Pinion   2006
Lettuce Shark   2215
Levant Blackneck   2296
Lewes Wave   1683

Lichen Case-bearer   179
Light Arches   2322
Light Brocade   2157
Light Brown Apple Moth   998
Light Crimson Underwing   2454
Light Emerald   1961
Light Feathered Dart   2084
Light Grey Tortrix   1024
Light Knot Grass   2286
Light Magpie   1886
Light Orange Underwing   1662
Lilac Beauty   1910
Lime Hawk-moth   1979
Lime-speck Pug   1825

Ling Pug   1831
Little Emerald   1674
Little Thorn   1901

Lobster Moth   1999
Local Long-tailed Satin   2023
Locust Bean Moth   1460
Long-tailed Blue   1567

Lulworth Skipper   1528
Lunar Double-stripe   2456
Lunar Hornet Moth   371
Lunar Marbled Brown   2015
Lunar Thorn   1918
Lunar Underwing   2270
Lunar Yellow Underwing   2108
Lunar-spotted Pinion   2319

Lychnis   2173
Lyme Grass   2348

M

Magpie   1884
Maiden's Blush   1680
Mallow   1745
Mallow Skipper   1533
Manchester Treble-bar   1866
Many-lined   1741
Maori   2210
Maple Prominent   2009
Maple Pug   1812
Map-winged Swift   18
Marbled Beauty   2293
Marbled Brown   2014
Marbled Clover   2401
Marbled Coronet   2171
Marbled Green   2295
Marbled Grey   2294
Marbled Minor   2337
Marbled Orchard Tortrix   1083
Marbled Pug   1818
Marbled Tuffet   2426
Marbled White   1620
Marbled White Spot   2410
March Moth   1663
Marsh Carpet   1810
Marsh Dagger   2285
Marsh Fritillary   1610
Marsh Mallow Moth   2363
Marsh Moth   2392
Marsh Oblique-barred   2485

Marsh Pug   1822
Mathew's Wainscot   2200
May Highflyer   1778
Mazarine Blue   1578

Meadow Brown   1626
Meal Moth   1417
Mediterranean Brocade   2386
Mediterranean Flour Moth   1475
Mediterranean Fritillary   1609
Mediterranean Hawk-moth   1988
Mere Wainscot   2349
Mere's Pug   1827
Merveille du Jour   2247

Middle Lace Border   1686
Middle-barred Minor   2340
Milkweed   1630
Miller   2280
Minor Shoulder-knot   2225

Mocha   1676
Monarch   1630
Moorland Clouded Yellow   1542
Morris's Wainscot   2346
Mother of Pearl   1405
Mother Shipton   2462
Mottled Beauty   1941
Mottled Grey   1775
Mottled Pug   1819
Mottled Rustic   2387
Mottled Umber   1935
Mountain Ringlet   1617
Mouse Moth   2299

Mullein   2221
Mullein Wave   1689
Mung Moth   1401
Muslin Footman   2038
Muslin Moth   2063

N

Narrow-bordered Bee Hawk-
     moth   1982
Narrow-bordered Five-spot
     Burnet   171
Narrow-winged Pug   1846

Neglected Rustic   2132

Netted Carpet   1772
Netted Mountain Moth   1895
Netted Pug   1823
New Forest Burnet   168

Ni Moth   2432
Nine-spotted   2070
Niobe Fritillary   1605

Nonconformist   2239
Northern Arches   2324
Northern Brown Argus   1573
Northern Dart   2125
Northern Deep-brown Dart
     2231
Northern Drab   2184
Northern Footman   2048
Northern Ruby Tiger   2064
Northern Rustic   2104
Northern Spinach   1756
Northern Winter Moth   1800
November Moth   1795

Nun   2416
Nut Bud Moth   1139
Nut Leaf Blister Moth   342
Nutmeg   2145
Nut-tree Tussock   2425

O

Oak Beauty   1930
Oak Eggar   1637
Oak Hook-tip   1646
Oak Lutestring   1658
Oak Nycteoline   2423
Oak Processionary   2022
Oak-tree Pug   1853

Oberthür's Grizzled Skipper
     1535
Oblique Carpet   1719
Oblique Striped   1718
Obscure Wainscot   2204

Ochraceous Wave   1697
Ochreous Pug   1844

Old Lady   2300

Oleander Hawk-moth   1985
Olive   2312
Olive Crescent   2495

Orache Moth   2304
Orange Footman   2043
Orange Moth   1924
Orange Sallow   2271
Orange Swift   15
Orange Underwing   1661
Orange Upperwing   2257
Orange-tailed Clearwing   378
Orange-tip   1553
Orchard Ermine   425
Oriental Fruit Moth   1248

P

Paignton Snout   2479
Painted Lady   1591
Painted Meal Moth   1419
Pale Brindled Beauty   1926
Pale Clouded Yellow   1543
Pale Eggar   1632
Pale Mottled Willow   2389
Pale November Moth   1796
Pale Oak Beauty   1944
Pale Pinion   2236
Pale Prominent   2011
Pale Shining Brown   2148
Pale Stigma   2141
Pale Tussock   2028
Pale-lemon Sallow   2276
Pale-shouldered Brocade   2158
Parsnip Moth   672
Pauper Pug   1824

Pea Moth   1257
Peach Blossom   1652
Peach Twig Borer   857
Peacock   1597
Peacock Moth   1889
Pear Leaf Blister Moth   260
Pearl-bordered Fritillary   1601
Pearly Underwing   2119
Pease Blossom   2398
Pebble Hook-tip   1648
Pebble Prominent   2003
Peppered Moth   1931

Phoenix   1754

Pigmy Footman   2046
Pimpinel Pug   1845
Pine Beauty   2179
Pine Bud Moth   1209
Pine Carpet   1767
Pine Hawk-moth   1978
Pine Leaf-mining Moth   1207
Pine Processionary   2021
Pine Resin-gall Moth   1214
Pine Shoot Moth   1210
Pine-tree Lappet   1639
Pinion-spotted Pug   1820
Pinion-streaked Snout   2484
Pink-barred Sallow   2273
Pink-spotted Hawk-moth   1971
Pistol Case-bearer   533

Plain Clay   2103
Plain Golden Y   2443
Plain Pug   1842
Plain Wave   1715
Plum Fruit Moth   1247
Plum Tortrix   1082
Plumed Prominent   2013

Pod Lover   2167
Poplar Grey   2278
Poplar Hawk-moth   1981
Poplar Kitten   1998
Poplar Lutestring   1655
Portland Moth   2099
Portland Ribbon Wave   1714
Potato Tuber Moth   825
Powdered Quaker   2186
Powdered Rustic   2383

Pretty Chalk Carpet   1784
Pretty Marbled   2411
Pretty Pinion   1806
Privet Hawk-moth   1976

Purple Bar   1752
Purple Clay   2122
Purple Cloud   2097
Purple Emperor   1585
Purple Hairstreak   1557
Purple Marbled   2407
Purple Thorn   1919
Purple Treble-bar   1869
Purple-barred Yellow   1717
Purple-bordered Gold   1698
Purple-edged Copper   1566
Purple-shaded Gem   2438
Purple-shot Copper   1565

Puss Moth   1995

Q

Queen of Spain Fritillary   1603

R

Raisin Moth   1477
Rannoch Brindled Beauty   1929
Rannoch Looper   1896
Rannoch Sprawler   2228
Raspberry Moth   136

Red Admiral   1590
Red Carpet   1723
Red Chestnut   2139
Red Sword-grass   2241
Red Twin-spot Carpet   1724
Red Underwing   2452
Red-barred Tortrix   1010
Red-belted Clearwing   379
Reddish Buff   2393
Reddish Light Arches   2323
Red-green Carpet   1760
Red-headed Chestnut   2261
Red-line Quaker   2263
Red-necked Footman   2039
Red-tipped Clearwing   380
Reed Dagger   2290
Reed Leopard   160
Reed Tussock   2024
Rest Harrow   1664

Rhomboid Tortrix   1042

Riband Wave   1713
Rice Moth   1427
Ringed Carpet   1939
Ringed China-mark   1348
Ringlet   1629
Rivulet   1802

Rose Leaf Miner   92
Rose Tortrix   981
Rosy Footman   2037
Rosy Marbled   2396
Rosy Marsh Moth   2115
Rosy Minor   2342

Rosy Rustic   2361
Rosy Underwing   2453
Rosy Wave   1691
Round-winged Muslin   2035
Royal Mantle   1736

Ruby Tiger   2064
Ruddy Carpet   1735
Ruddy Highflyer   1779
Rufous Minor   2338
Rush Veneer   1398
Rush Wainscot   2374
Rustic Shoulder-knot   2334
Rusty Wave   1703

S

Sallow   2274
Sallow Clearwing   377
Sallow Kitten   1997
Sallow Nycteoline   2424
Saltern Ear   2358
Sand Dart   2093
Sandhill Rustic   2354
Sandy Carpet   1808
Satellite   2256
Satin Beauty   1940
Satin Lutestring   1656
Satin Wave   1709
Satyr Pug   1828

Scalloped Hazel   1920
Scalloped Hook-tip   1645
Scalloped Oak   1921
Scalloped Shell   1789
Scar Bank Gem   2430
Scarce Arches   2356
Scarce Black Arches   2079
Scarce Blackneck   2467
Scarce Bordered Straw   2400
Scarce Brindle   2328
Scarce Burnished Brass   2435
Scarce Chocolate-tip   2018
Scarce Copper   1563
Scarce Dagger   2287
Scarce Footman   2047
Scarce Forester   165
Scarce Hook-tip   1650
Scarce Marbled   2409
Scarce Meal-moth   2406
Scarce Merveille du Jour   2277
Scarce Prominent   2010
Scarce Pug   1847

Scarce Silver-lines   2421
Scarce Silver Y   2447
Scarce Swallowtail   1540
Scarce Tissue   1788
Scarce Tortoiseshell   1595
Scarce Umber   1933
Scarce Vapourer   2025
Scarce Wormwood   2213
Scarlet Tiger   2068
Scorched Carpet   1888
Scorched Wing   1904
Scotch Annulet   1963
Scotch Argus   1618
Scotch Burnet   166

Seathorn Hawk-moth   1989
September Thorn   1915
Seraphim   1879
Setaceous Hebrew Character
   2126

Shaded Broad-bar   1732
Shaded Pug   1840
Shark   2216
Sharp-angled Carpet   1794
Sharp-angled Peacock   1890
Shears   2147
Shore Wainscot   2201
Short-cloaked Moth   2077
Short-tailed Blue   1570
Shoulder Stripe   1746
Shoulder-striped Clover   2402
Shoulder-striped Wainscot   2205
Shuttle-shaped Dart   2092

Silky Wainscot   2391
Silky Wave   1704
Silurian   2175
Silver Barred   2413
Silver Cloud   2181
Silver Hook   2412
Silver Y   2441
Silver-ground Carpet   1727
Silver-spotted Skipper   1529
Silver-striped Hawk-moth   1993
Silver-studded Blue   1571
Silver-washed Fritillary   1608
Silvery Arches   2149
Single-dotted Wave   1708
Six-belted Clearwing   382
Six-spot Burnet   169
Six-striped Rustic   2133

Skin Moth   227

Slate Flash   1560
Slender Brindle   2335
Slender Burnished Brass   2433
Slender Pug   1811
Slender Scotch Burnet   167
Slender-striped Rufous   1780
Sloe Carpet   1959
Sloe Pug   1859

Small Angle Shades   2305
Small Apollo   1537
Small Argent & Sable   1737
Small Autumnal Moth   1798
Small Black Arches   2075
Small Blood-vein   1690
Small Blue   1569
Small Brindled Beauty   1925
Small Brown Shoemaker   1589
Small China-mark   1354
Small Chocolate-tip   2017
Small Clouded Brindle   2331
Small Clover Case-bearer   517
Small Copper   1561
Small Dark Yellow Underwing
   2143
Small Dotted Buff   2345
Small Dotted Footman   2042
Small Dusty Wave   1707
Small Eggar   1633
Small Elephant Hawk-moth
   1992
Small Emerald   1673
Small Engrailed   1948
Small Fan-foot   2492
Small Fan-footed Wave   1702
Small Grass Emerald   1670
Small Heath   1627
Small Lappet   1641
Small Magpie   1376
Small Marbled   2408
Small Mottled Willow   2385
Small Pearl-bordered Fritillary
   1600
Small Phoenix   1759
Small Purple-barred   2470
Small Quaker   2182
Small Ranunculus   2165
Small Rivulet   1803
Small Rufous   2379
Small Scallop   1712
Small Seraphim   1882
Small Skipper   1526
Small Square-spot   2123
Small Tabby   1420
Small Tortoiseshell   1594
Small Wainscot   2350

Small Waved Umber 1781
Small White 1550
Small White Wave 1875
Small Yellow Underwing 2397
Small Yellow Wave 1876
Smoky Wainscot 2198
Smoky Wave 1694

Snout 2477

Sooty Copper 1564
Southern Wainscot 2197

Spanish Carpet 1730
Spanish Festoon 1538
Speckled Beauty 1946
Speckled Footman 2053
Speckled Wood 1614
Speckled Yellow 1909
Spectacle 2450
Spinach 1757
Spindle Ermine 427
Spiny Bollworm 2419
Spotted Clover Moth 2405
Spotted Fritillary 1611
Spotted Shoot Moth 1212
Spotted Sulphur 2414
Sprawler 2227
Spring Usher 1932
Spruce Carpet 1769
Spurge Hawk-moth 1986

Square Spot 1949
Square-spot Dart 2080
Square-spot Rustic 2134
Square-spotted Clay 2131

Star-wort 2217
Stephen's Gem 2445
Stored Nut Moth 1430
Stout Dart 2113
Strange Wave 1700
Stranger 2161
Straw Belle 1967
Straw Dot 2474
Straw Underwing 2303
Strawberry Tortrix 1037
Streak 1864
Streaked Wave 1685
Streamer 1747
Striped Hawk-moth 1990
Striped Lychnis 2219

Striped Twin-spot Carpet 1753
Striped Wainscot 2196

Sub-angled Wave 1684
Summer Fruit Tortrix 999
Suspected 2268
Sussex Emerald 1672

Svensson's Copper Underwing
  2298

Swallow Prominent 2007
Swallowtail 1539
Swallow-tailed Moth 1922
Sweet Gale Moth 2288
Sword-grass 2242

Sycamore 2279

T

Tamarisk Pug 1850
Tapestry Moth 234
Tawny Marbled Minor 2339
Tawny Pinion 2235
Tawny Shears 2167
Tawny Shoulder 2096
Tawny Speckled Pug 1838
Tawny Wave 1688
Tawny-barred Angle 1893

Tea Tabby 1422

Thistle Ermine 1458
Three-humped Prominent 2002
Thrift Clearwing 383
Thyme Moth 820
Thyme Pug 1843

Timothy Tortrix 989
Tissue 1790

Toadflax Brocade 2223
Toadflax Pug 1816
Tomato Sphinx 1975

Transparent Burnet   172
Treble Brown Spot   1711
Treble Lines   2380
Treble-bar   1867
Tree-lichen Beauty   2292
Triangle   174
Triple-barred   2459
Triple-spotted Clay   2127
Triple-spotted Pug   1826
Tropical Tobacco Moth   209
True Lover's Knot   2118

Tunbridge Wells Gem   2429
Turnip Moth   2087
Turquoise Blue   1577

Twenty-plume Moth   1288
Twin-spot Carpet   1809
Twin-spotted Quaker   2189
Twin-spotted Tabby   2487
Twin-spotted Wainscot   2370

U

Uncertain   2381
Union Rustic   2332

V

Valerian Pug   1821
Vapourer   2026
Varied Coronet   2170
Variegated Golden Tortrix   980

Vestal   1716

Vine Moth   955
Vine's Rustic   2384
Viper's Bugloss   2168

V-Moth   1897

V-Pug   1858

W

Wall   1615
Water Betony   2220

Water Carpet   1750
Water Ermine   2062
Water Veneer   1331
Waved Black   2475
Waved Carpet   1877
Waved Tabby   2486
Waved Umber   1936
Wax Moth   1425

Weaver's Fritillary   1602
Weaver's Wave   1710
Webb's Wainscot   2373
Welsh Clearwing   376
Welsh Wave   1873

White Admiral   1584
White Colon   2152
White Ermine   2060
White Letter Hairstreak   1558
White Plume Moth   1513
White Prominent   2012
White Satin Moth   2031
White Spot   2172
   Hadena albimaculata
White Spot   1898
   Hypagyrtis unipunctata
White-banded Carpet   1786
White-barred Clearwing   375
White-line Dart   2018
White-line Snout   2482
White-mantled Wainscot   2372
White-marked   2140
White-pinion Spotted   1957
White-point   2194
White-shouldered House-moth
   648
White-speck   2203
White-spotted Pinion   2317
White-spotted Pug   1835

Wild Cherry Sphinx   1977
Willow Beauty   1937
Willow Ermine   428
Willow Tortrix   1147
Winter Moth   1799

Wood Tiger   2056
Wood White   1541
Woodland Grayling   1622
Wormwood   2211
Wormwood Pug   1830

Y

Yarrow Pug   1841

Yellow Belle   1968
Yellow Horned   1659
Yellow Shell   1742
Yellow V Moth   277
Yellow-barred Brindle   1883
Yellow-legged Clearwing   374
Yellow-line Quaker   2264
Yellow-ringed Carpet   1743
Yellow-tail   2030

Yorkshire Y   2448

Z

Zebra   1588

ABBREVIATIONS OF AUTHORS' NAMES

Adamcz.   Adamczewski
Agass.   Agassiz
Bar.   Barasch
Barr.   Barrett
Ben.   Benander
Bent.   Bentinck
Billb.   Billberg
Bjerk.   Bjerkander
Blanch.   Blanchard
Blesz.   Bleszynski
Boh.   Boheman
Bohem.   Boheman
Boisd.   Boisduval
Borkh.   Borkhausen
Bours.   Boursin
Bradl.   Bradley
Bru.   Bruand
Brünn.   Brünnich
Brem. & Grey   Bremer & Grey
Burr.   Burrows
Butl.   Butler
Bütt.   Büttner
Byt.-Salz   Bytinski-Salz
Carad.   Caradja
C.-Hunt   Chalmers-Hunt
Chrét.   Chrétien
Christ.   Christoph
Cl.   Clerck
Clem.   Clemens
Cock.   Cockayne
Cockll.   Cockerell
Const.   Constant
Corb. & Tams   Corbet & Tams
Curt.   Curtis
Cyr.   Cyrillo
D. & S.   Denis & Schiffermüller
Dalm.   Dalman
De G.   De Geer
Desv.   Desvignes
Diak.   Diakonoff
Diak. & Hepp.   Diakonoff & Heppner
Diak. & Hint.   Diakonoff & Hinton
Don.   Donovan
Doubl.   Doubleday
Dougl.   Douglas
Dup.   Duponchel
Durr.   Durrant
Edw.   Edwards
Esp.   Esper
Fabr.   Fabricius
Falk.   Falkovitsh
Fletch.   Fletcher
Fol.   Fologne
Forst.   Forster

```
Freem.    Freeman
Fröl.    Frölich
Fruh.    Fruhstorfer
Fuess.    Fuessly
Fuessl.    Fuessly
F.v.R.    Fischer von Rösslerstamm
Geoff.    Geoffroy
Geoffr.    Geoffroy in Fourcroy
Germ.    Germar
Goods.    Goodson
Gozm.    Gozmány
Grasl.    Graslin
Greg. & Pov.    Gregor & Povolný
Gregs.    Gregson
Guen.    Guenée
H.-S.    Herrich-Schäffer
Hamps.    Hampson
Hann.    Hannemann
Hard.    Hardwick
Harr.    Harrison
Haw.    Haworth
Hb.    Hübner
Hein.    Heinemann
Heinr.    Heinrich
Hemm.    Hemming
Her.    Hering
Herb.    Herbulot
Heyd.    Heyden
Heyl.    Heylaerts
Hodgk.    Hodgkinson
Hofm.    Hofmann
Hohen.    Hohenwarth
How.    Howarth
Hufn.    Hufnagel
Hum.    Hummel
Humph. & West.    Humphreys & Westwood
Ill. & Hof.    Illiger & Hoffmannsegg
Jerm.    Jermyn
Joan.    Joannis
Johan.    Johansson
Jord.    Jordan
Karsh. & Niel.    Karshalt & Nielsen
Kearf.    Kearfott
Kenn.    Kennel
Kiriak    Kiriakoff
Klim.    Klimesch
Koll.    Koller
Kostr.    Kostrowicki
Krog.    Krogerus
Lam.    Lamarck
Lasp.    Laspeyres
Lat.    Latreille
Latr.    Latreille
Latt.    de Lattin
Led.    Lederer
Lefeb.    Lefebvre
Lien. & Zell.    Lienig & Zeller
```

Linn.   Linnaeus
Mab.   Mabille
Mart.   Martini
McDunn.   McDunnough
McLach.   McLachan
Meig.   Meigen
Metc.   Metcalfe
Meyr.   Meyrick
Mill.   Millier
Mühl.   Mühlig
Müll.   Müller
Müll.-Rutz   Müller-Rutz
Munr.   Munroe
Newm.   Newman
Nic.   Nicelli
Nolck.   Nolcken
Now.   Nowicki
Nyl.   Nylander
Obraz.   Obraztsov
Obraz. & Swats.   Obraztsov & Swatschek
Ochs.   Ochsenheimer
Ol.   Olivier
Osb.   Osbeck
Pack.   Packard
Palm.   Palmer
Panz.   Panzer
Pel.-Clint.   Pelham-Clinton
Pet.   Petersen
Pfaff.   Pfaffenzeller
Philp.   Philpott
Pier.   Pierret
Pier. & Metc.   Pierce & Metcalf
Pill.   Piller
Pop.-G. & Cap.   Popescu-Georg & Capuse
Pov.   Povolny
Preis.   Preissecker
Raf.   Rafinesque
Rag.   Ragonot
Ramb.   Rambur
Ratz.   Ratzeburg
Retz.   Retzius
Rich.   Richardson
R.L.   Full name not known
Roem.   Roemer
Rössl.   Rössler
Roths.   Rothschild
Rott.   Rottenburg
Rowl.-Br.   Rowland-Brown
Sam.   Samoulle
Sattl.   Sattler
Schäff.   Schäffer
Scharf.   Scharfenburg
Schaw.   Schawerda
Schev.   Scheven
Schl.   Schleich
Schläg.   Schläger
Schr.   Schrank

```
Schreb.      Schreber
Scop.        Scopoli
Scudd.       Scudder
Sheld.       Sheldon
Sirc.        Sircom
Snell.       Snellen
Sodof.       Sodoffsky
Sorh.        Sorhagen
Spey.        Speyer
Spul.        Spuler
Stdgr        Staudinger
Steph.       Stephens
Steud.       Steudel
Stt.         Stainton
Sukh.        Sukhareva
Svens.       Svensson
Swinh.       Swindhoe
Tausch.      Tauscher
Tengst.      Tengström
Thomps.      Thompson
Threl.       Threlfall
Thunb.       Thunberg
Thunb. & Beck.     Thunberg & Becklin
Treit.       Treitschke
Trem.        Tremewan
Tr.-O. & Niel.    Traugatt-Olsen & Nielsen
Turn.        Turner
Urb.         Urbahn
Vaugh.       Vaughan
Ver.         Verity
View.        Vieweg
Vill.        Villers
Walk.        Walker
Wall.        Wallengren
Wals.        Walsingham
Warr.        Warren
Watk.        Watkins
Werneb.      Werneburg
Westw.       Westwood
Will.        Williams
Wnuk.        Wnukowsky
Woll.        Wollaston
W.P. Curt.   Parkinson-Curtis
Zag.         Zagulaer
Zell.        Zeller
Zett.        Zetterstedt
Zinck.       Zincken
```

From Addenda & Corrigenda

```
Enderl.      Enderlein
Luc.         Lucas
```

ADDENDA AND CORRIGENDA

Compiled by J.D. Bradley & D.S. Fletcher

The following amendments include 15 species added to the British list since publication of the "Log Book" in 1979.

34	occultella Linn. *argentipedella* Zell.	....
216a	inconditella Luc. *heydeni* Pet.	....
222	arcuatella Stt. *laterella* Thunb. nec D. & S.	....
229	obviella D. & S. *ferruginella* Hb. nec Thunb.	....
237	fuscella Linn. *fuscipunctella* Haw.	....
260	malifoliella Costa *scitella* Zell. Pear Leaf Blister Moth	....

below *386
PROCHOREUTIS Diak. & Hepp.
CHOREUTIS auct.

below 388
CHOREUTIS Hb.
EUTROMULA Fröl.

*409a	trifasciata Stdgr	....
412	pygmaeella D. & S.	....
421	bonnetella Linn. *curvella* Linn.	....
437a	passerella Zett. *nanivora* Stt.	....
465a	haasi Stdgr	....
476	autumnitella Curt. *pygmeana* Haw. nec Hb.	....
496a	adjectella H.-S.	....
556a	linosyridella Fuchs	....
557	gardesanella Toll *machinella* Bradl.	....
565	saxicolella Dup. *benanderi* Kanerva	....

574	deviella Zell.	....
	suaedivora Meyr.	
607	obscurella Stt.	....
	pulchella Haw. nec Fabr.	
616a	littoricola Le March	....

below 664
DASYSTOMA   Curt.
CHEIMOPHILA   auct.

680	aegopodiella Hb.	....
	albipunctella Hb. nec D. & S.	
695	alstromeriana Cl.	....
	alstroemeriana misspell.	
703	atomella D. & S.	....
	pulverella Hb.	
705	ulicetella Stt.	....
	prostratella Const.	
707	Now synonymised with 705	
727a	aprilella H.-S.	....

below 760
ATHRIPS   Billb.
RHYNCHOPACHA   Stdgr

871a	caradjai Pop.-G. & Cap.	....
	bifasciella sensu Steph.	
920a	inspersella Hb.	....

above 921
TRACHYSMIA   Guen.
HYSTEROSIA   Steph.

below 934
COCHYLIMORPHA   Raz.
STENODES   Guen. nec Duj.

1138	nisella Cl.	....
	nisella Cl.	
	f. cinereana Haw.	....
1151	trigonella Linn.	....
	stroemiana Fabr.	
1191	catoptrana Rebel	....
	heringiana Jäckh	

*1203   torridana Led.   . . . .
*1203   *hastana* sensu Hb.

below 1213
        RETINA Guen.
        PETROVA Heinr.

1227   inquilina Fletch.   . . . .
        inquilana misspell.

1301   lathoniellus Zinck.   . . . .
        nemorella Hb. nec Thunb.

1338   lacustrata Panz.   . . . .
        crataegella auct.

1343   delunella Stt.   . . . .
        vandaliella H.-S.
        resinella auct.

*1347a   manilensis Hamps.   . . . .

*1351a   fluctuosalis Zell.   . . . .

*1351b   crisonalis Walk.   . . . .
        stagnalis sensu Agass.

1388   lutealis Hb.   . . . .
        elutalis auct.

*1409   hyalinata Linn.   . . . .
        lucernalis Hb.

below *1411
        SCELIODES Guen.
        DARABA Walk.

1454a   schuetzeella Fuchs   . . . .

below 1464
        ZOPHODIA Hb.

*1464a   grossulariella Hb.   . . . .
        convolutella auct.

1485   maritima Tengst.   . . . .
        carlinella Hein.

below *1649
        SABRA Bode
        SABRE auct.

below *1717
        PHIBALAPTERYX Steph.
        MESOTYPE acut.

1769	britannica Turn.	....
	variata auct.	
	Spruce Carpet	
1923	pennaria Linn.	....
1937a	secundaria Esp.	....

below 1948 insert
      PARADARISA Warr.

below 2026
      DICALLOMERA Butl.
      DASYCHIRA auct.

above 2028 insert
      CALLITEARA Butl.
      DASYCHIRA auct.

| 2205 | comma Linn. | .... |

below 2399 insert
      HELIOTHIS Ochs.

and delete
      HELICOVERPA Hard.

below 2400 delete
      HELIOTHIS Ochs.

| 2435 | chryson Esp. | .... |

Listed below are further additions to ADDENDA AND CORRIGENDA that were received just before going to press. No account has been taken of them in either the main index or that on page 37.

below 175
      DAHLICA Enderl.
      SOLENOBIA auct.

below 180
      TALEPORIA Hb.
      SOLENOBIA Dup.

| 393 | equitella Scop. | .... |
| | *minorella* Snell. | |